THE DEAD SEA SCROLLS

MAJOR PUBLICATIONS AND TOOLS FOR STUDY

JOSEPH A. FITZMYER, S.J.

SOURCES FOR BIBLICAL STUDY 8
Society of Biblical Literature
and
SCHOLARS PRESS

Distributed by

SCHOLARS PRESS
University of Montana
Missoula, Montana 59801

Library of Congress Cataloging in Publication Data

Fitzmyer, Joseph A
The Dead Sea scrolls--major publications and tools for study.

(Sources for Biblical study ; 8)
Bibliography: p.
1. Dead Sea scrolls--Bibliography. I. Title. II. Series
Z6371.D4F58 [BM487] [016.2214'4] 75-5987
ISBN 0-88414-053-9

Printed in the United States of America

Printing Department
University of Montana
Missoula, Montana 59801

TABLE OF CONTENTS

Page

GENERAL ABBREVIATIONS

ADAJ	*Annual of the Department of Antiquities of Jordan*
ALQ	Cross, F. M., Jr., *The Ancient Library of Qumran* (see p. 61)
ALUOS	*Annual of Leeds University Oriental Society*
ASTI	*Annual of the Swedish Theological Institute*
BA	*Biblical Archaeologist*
BASOR	*Bulletin of the American Schools of Oriental Research*
BBB	Bonner biblische Beiträge
Bib	*Biblica*
BIES	*Bulletir of the Israel Exploration Society* (later renamed *Yedi'ot*)
BZAW	Beihefte zur *ZAW*
BZNW	Beihefte zur *ZNW*
CBQ	*Catholic Biblical Quarterly*
DJD	Discoveries in the Judaean Desert (of Jordan)
DSSHU	E. L. Sukenik, *The Dead Sea Scrolls of the Hebrew University* (see p. 12)
DSPS	J. A. Sanders, *The Dead Sea Psalms Scroll* (see p. 35)
DTT	*Dansk Teologisk Tidsskrift*
ESBNT	J. A. Fitzmyer, *Essays on the Semitic Background of the New Testament* (London: Chapman, 1971; paperback, Missoula: Scholars' Press, 1974)
EstEcl	*Estudios eclesiásticos*
EvQ	*Evangelical Quarterly*
EvT	*Evangelische Theologie*
ExpT	*Expository Times*
FRLANT	Forschungen zur Religion und Literatur des Alten und Neuen Testamentes
HTR	*Harvard Theological Review*
HTS	Harvard Theological Studies
IEJ	*Israel Exploration Journal*
ILN	*Illustrated London News*
JBL	*Journal of Biblical Literature*
JEOL	*Jaarbericht ex oriente lux*
JJS	*Journal of Jewish Studies*

JQR	*Jewish Quarterly Review*
JSJ	*Journal for the Study of Judaism*
JSS	*Journal of Semitic Studies*
JTC	*Journal for Theology and the Church*
JTS	*Journal of Theological Studies*
NAB	*The New American Bible* (Paterson, NJ: St. Anthony Guild, 1970)
NDBA	*New Directions in Biblical Archaeology* (eds. D. N. Freedman and J. C. Greenfield; Garden City: Doubleday, 1969)
NRT	*La nouvelle revue théologique*
NTS	*New Testament Studies*
OS	*Oudtestamentische Studiën*
PEQ	*Palestine Exploration Quarterly*
RB	*Revue biblique*
RechBib	Recherches bibliques
REJ	*Revue des études juives*
RHPR	*Revue d'histoire et de philosophie religieuses*
RHR	*Revue de l'histoire des religions*
RQ	*Revue de Qumran*
SBFLA	*Studii biblici franciscani liber annuus*
SBT	Studies in Biblical Theology
STDJ	Studies on the Texts of the Desert of Judah
SP	*Studia papyrologica*
SWDS	*Scrolls from the Wilderness of the Dead Sea* (Smithsonian Institution Exhibit Catalogue; Cambridge: American Schools of Oriental Research, 1965)
TLZ	*Theologische Literaturzeitung*
TS	*Theological Studies*
TU	Texte und Untersuchungen
USQR	*Union Seminary Quarterly Review*
VT	*Vetus Testamentum*
VTSup	Vetus Testamentum, Supplements (Leiden: Brill)
WTJ	*Westminster Theological Journal*
WUNT	Wissenschaftliche Untersuchungen zum Neuen Testament
ZAW	*Zeitschrift für die alttestamentliche Wissenschaft*

ZDPV	*Zeitschrift des deutschen Palästina-Vereins*
ZNW	*Zeitschrift für die neutestamentliche Wissenschaft*
ZTK	*Zeitschrift für Theologie und Kirche*

(Abbreviations of the names of biblical books, apocrypha, pseudepigrapha, and early patristic writings follow the system proposed in *JBL* 90 [1971] 513-14.)

FOREWORD

The student who undertakes to study the Dead Sea Scrolls soon realizes the vastness of this modern aspect of biblical studies. The bearing of the discovery of these texts on the technical study of the Bible is far from having been exploited. To some the topic of the Dead Sea Scrolls may seem to be "old hat," but when one realizes that we are still waiting for the publication of about 95 per cent of the texts from Qumran Cave 4 alone, then it is evident that much important material is still to be brought to light and that the full bearing of this remarkable manuscript discovery on texts of the Old and New Testament is still to be worked out. Many are the aspects of the study of the Dead Sea Scrolls, for they contain not only forms of the texts of the Greek, Hebrew, and Aramaic Scriptures, but also much other Palestinian Jewish literature of the last two centuries BC and of the first century AD. They bear upon the history and archaeology of the Roman period of Palestine. And the pertinence of them in providing a Palestinian Jewish background for many NT writings is far from having been adequately assessed.

In many graduate or divinity schools with programs devoted to biblical studies or to the study of the Northwest Semitic languages, seminars are often conducted in the reading and interpretation of the Qumran scrolls. The first problem that confronts students in such seminars is all too frequently that of trying to find out where the texts to be studied have actually been published, either in a definitive or a preliminary form, and where one must go for the secondary literature on them. For many of them have been published in partial or preliminary forms in out-of-the-way places, in different periodicals or in *Festschriften*, and it is not easy to keep track of them.

Moreover, the very term "Dead Sea Scrolls" is used today in different ways. In a *generic* sense it often embraces texts coming from discoveries during the last quarter of a century at different sites along the northwest shore of the Dead Sea. In a *specific* sense, however, it is restricted to the Qumran scrolls, texts written in Hebrew, Aramaic, or Greek on papyrus and skin which were found in (to date) eleven caves in the vicinity of Ḫirbet Qumran. But in the wider generic sense the term is often used to include the texts found at Masada, Wadi Murabbaʿat, Naḥal Ḥever, Naḥal Ṣeʾelim, Ṇahal Mishmar, Ḫirbet Mird, and even (in a few instances) texts from the Cairo Genizah.

In an effort to sort out all this material, to explain the various sigla used for it, to indicate the places of publication of the Dead Sea Scroll material made available to date, to explain the contents of the texts, and to introduce the student to various tools of study, this compilation has been made. It includes not only the list of sites where the texts have been found and the full bibliographical titles of the major publications, but also guides to further material: bibliographies of the Dead Sea Scrolls, survey articles, other attempts to list the material, concordances and dictionaries for the study of the texts, secondary collections of Qumran texts, translations in modern languages, outlines of the more important, longer Qumran texts, and some of the more important bibliography on selected topics of scroll-study or secondary literature about them.

An effort has been made to be exhaustive in the listing of the sites and the texts that have been published to date which come from them. But when it comes to the secondary bibliography on the topics treated, no effort has been made to be exhaustive. These bibliographies are selective, and it is to be hoped that at least the more important material is represented among them and that it will provide leads to further material. In the case of the select bibliographies there is always room for a critic's one-up-manship. However, reviewers of this work are seriously asked for the references to significant contributions that may be lacking in these sections.

The eight sites that are treated here have a certain coherence, either because of the time of the discoveries or because of the period which they represent. Texts such as those of the Wadi ed-Daliyeh have not been included, because, although they may come from a site not too far away from Ḫirbet Qumran, they really have nothing to do with the period in question. One might wonder why the texts from Ḫirbet Mird were included. That is solely because of the time of their discovery and of the association of them in the popular mind with the so-called Dead Sea Scrolls. They are included only to sort them out from the rest.

A word should be said about the decision to include outlines of some of the important texts. The outlines are to a certain extent subjective; others may prefer other ways of outlining the texts. But since most of the material in this volume has grown out of an introductory course in the Dead Sea Scrolls, which I have been giving over the last few years, I have learned the value of supplying students with outlines of the longer texts that have to be read. They are included here, therefore, for their propaedeutic value as tools for study. There is, however, another aspect of them that should be mentioned: the outlines are not uniform. This is dictated by the nature of the texts outlined. In some instances one can only list the contents (e.g., 11QPs^{a} -- a bare list of the biblical and apocryphal psalms as well as the prose insertions). Yet even such a list provides a ready reference for the contents of that scroll; with it one can tell immediately whether a given psalm in the canonical psalter is present in the text of the Psalms scroll of Qumran Cave 11. The same is true of other problematic scrolls. Finally, the detailed list of the contents of scrolls is intended to facilitate the study of them from various standpoints (e.g., to enable one to check quickly for the Qumran texts in which some biblical book or other may be cited or used).

Full information (complete title, place of publication, publisher, etc.) is normally given only at the first occurrence. After that a brief title is used, but in the case of references to periodicals the volume number, year, and pertinent pages are included in subsequent references (after the first full listing of the information).

The reader should be aware that the sigla are not always followed by all students of, or commentators on, the Dead Sea Scrolls. Some still use the older system (see p. 8), which really should be abandoned; some who write in other modern languages sometimes use forms that are conventional to them. Thus, 11QtgHiob will not be found in the list below. Here one has to realize that the name for the Book of Job in German is different from the English name. And there are other, similar variants. An effort has been made to use the sigla that are current in English writings.

Finally, my thanks are due to Professor James A. Sanders, of Union Theological Seminary in New York, for his constructive criticism of an earlier draft of this work, and to Professor Wayne A. Meeks, of Yale University, the editor of the Sources for Biblical Study, for acceptance of it into this series. To the typist, Joann Burnich, who has done such an excellent job of typing this difficult manuscript, my thanks have to be expressed in a very special way. I must also thank Melissa A. Keith for her help in the preparation of the indexes.

1

THE SYSTEM OF ABBREVIATION USED FOR THE DEAD SEA SCROLLS

THE SYSTEM OF ABBREVIATION USED FOR THE DEAD SEA SCROLLS

(Cf. J. T. Milik, "Table des sigles," *DJD* 1. 46-48)

The system that was first used, when only Qumran Cave 1 was known (see the abbreviations at the end of the list of those commonly used today, p. 8), soon became outmoded, especially when it was necessary to distinguish various Qumran caves and multiple copies of the same document found in the same cave. As a result a system was devised, which seems complicated but, once it is explained and studied, proves to be easily followed. Five elements can make up the siglum for a given text, but not all five are always used, since the first and the fifth are commonly omitted. But they become necessary at times. The five elements in the order in which they occur are: (1) the material on which the text is written; (2) the name of the site where the text was discovered -- its provenience; (3) the title of the work; (4) which copy of that work at the given site; (5) the language in which the text is written (since sometimes the same text is found in more than one language).

MATERIAL	PROVENIENCE	TITLE OF WORK
(skin)	Q (Qumran: 1Q, 2Q, 3Q, etc.)	Gen, Exod, Lev, Num, Deut, etc.
p, pap (papyrus)	Mas (Masada)	paleoLev (Leviticus copied in paleo-Hebrew script)
cu (copper)	Mur (Murabbaʿat)	LXXNum (Numbers in the "Septuagint" version)
o, os, ostr (ostracon)	Ḥev (Ḥever)	Samar (Samaritan version)
lign (wood)	Ṣe (Ṣeʾelim)	Phyl (Phylactery)
perg (parchment)	Miš (Mišmar)	pHos (Pešer [commentary of] Hosea)
		tgJob (targum [Aramaic translation] of Job)

PROVENIENCE	TITLE OF WORK
Mird (Ḫirbet Mird)	apGen (apocryphon [non-canonical, literary work] based on Gen)
C (Cairo Genizah)	Sir (Sirach, Ecclesiasticus)
	Tob (Tobit, Tobias)
	EpJer (Epistle of Jeremy)
	Jub (Jubilees)
	Hen (Enoch, 1 Enoch)
	TLevi (Testament of Levi)
	TNaph (Testament of Naphtali)
	(Sectarian Texts, see below)
	Instead of a title, a (boldface or italic) number is often used; it corresponds to the number of the text in the volumes of DJD. Thus:
	1QPhyl = 1Q*13* or 1Q**13**
	The name of an OT book may be preceded by paleo (= paleo-Hebrew script), LXX (= Old Greek version), or tg (= targum, or Aramaic version of the book) or Samar.

COPY OF WORK	LANGUAGE
Superscript letters following the title or the language	nothing or hebr (= Hebrew)
	ar, aram (Aramaic)
	arab (Arabic)
	cpa (Christian Palestinian Aramaic)
	gr (Greek)
	lat (Latin)
	nab (Nabatean)

N.B. Normally, arabic numbers are used for caves, columns and lines (sometimes writers use colons to separate the columns and lines, sometimes periods, sometimes commas -- there is no set rule here). However, in some *fragmentary texts*, when there are several fragments and they must be numbered separately within a work, the *columns* are then designated by lower-case roman numerals. Thus 1Q*27* 1 ii 25 (which means text 27 from Qumran Cave 1, fragment 1, column ii, line 25). In this case it is better not to use colons, periods, or commas. Similarly, 4QpIsa^{c} 4-7 ii 2-4 (which means the third copy [copy c] of a pesher on Isaiah from Qumran Cave 4 [cf. 4Q*163*; DJD 5. 17-27], joined fragments 4 to 7, column ii, lines 2 to 4).

Abbreviations Commonly Used in This System

ap	apocryphon
apoc	apocalypse
ar or aram	Aramaic
arab	Arabic
BA	Babatha Archive
BarC	Bar Cochba
Ben	Benediction(s)
Ber	B^{e}rākôt
C	Cairo (Genizah)
Cal	Calendar(ic)
col	column
cpa	Christian Palestinian Aramaic
Cryptic	Cryptic Astrological Text
cu	copper
D	Damascus Document
DibHam	Dibrê Hamm^{e}'ôrôt (= Paroles des Luminaires)
DM	Dires de Moïse (Sayings of Moses)
Ep	Epistle, Letter
EschMidr	Eschatological Midrash(im)
Flor(ilegium)	Florilegium
fr(s)	fragment(s)
gr	Greek
H	Hôdāyôt (= Thanksgiving Psalms)
hebr	Hebrew
Hen	Enoch
Ḥev	Ḥever (= Wadi Ḫabra)
Hym	Hymn(ic)
Jn or JerNouv	Jérusalem Nouvelle (= New Jerusalem)
Jub	Jubilees, Book of
lat	Latin
lign	wood (= lignum)
Lit	Liturgy, Liturgical
LXX	Septuagint
M	Milḥāmāh (War Scroll)
Mas	Masada

Melch	Melchizedek
Mess	Messianic (Text)
Mez	Mezuzah
Mird	Ḫirbet Mird
Mis	Mishmar (Naḥal Mishmar = Wadi Mahras)
MT	Masoretic Text
Mur	Murabbaʿât (Wadi)
nab	Nabatean
olim	formerly
o	ostracon
Ord	Ordinances
os	ostracon
p	pesher (= commentary); but sometimes it is used for pap
paleo	Text is written in Paleo-Hebrew script
palimp	palimpsest
paraph	paraphrase
pap	papyrus
PBless	Patriarchal Blessings
perg	parchment (= pergamentum)
Phyl	phylactery
Pr	Prayer(s)
PrNab	Prayer of Nabonidus
Proph	Prophecy, Prophetic
Ps(s)	Psalm(s), Psalter
PsAp	Apocryphal Psalms
Ps-	Pseudo-
Q	Qumran
Rit	Ritual
S	Serek Hay-yaḥad (= Manual of Discipline)
Sa	Appendix A to 1QS (= 1Q*28a*): Rule of the Congregation
Sb	Appendix B to 1QS (= 1Q*28b*): Collection of Benedictions

Sam	Samaritan
Ṣe	(Naḥal) Ṣe'elim (= Wadi Seiyal)
ŠirŠabb	Serek šîrôt 'ôlat haššabbāt (= Order of the Songs of the Sabbath Holocaust)
Sl 39-40	Strugnell Texts 39-40 (= Angelic Liturgy)
syr	Syriac
T	Testament
Testim	Testimonia
Tg	targum
Vis	Vision
XII	Twelve Minor Prophets
Wiles	Wiles of the Wicked Woman

Older System of Abbreviations

CDC	Cairo Damascus Covenant (= CD)
DSD	Dead Sea Discipline (= 1QS)
DSH	Dead Sea Habakkuk Commentary (= 1QpHab)
DSIa	Dead Sea Isaiah A (= 1QIsa[a])
DSIb	Dead Sea Isaiah B (= 1QIsa[b])
DSL	Dead Sea Lamech Apocalypse (= (= 1QapGen)
DST	Dead Sea Thanksgiving Psalms (= 1QH)
DSW	Dead Sea War Scroll (= 1QM)

[This older system should no longer be used. Even though it is simpler, it tends to confuse.]

2

THE DEAD SEA SCROLLS: MAJOR PUBLICATIONS

MAJOR PUBLICATIONS

In the following list can be found all the places in which various Dead Sea Scrolls have been published. It contains not only the *editio princeps* but also the preliminary or partial publications, which contain all of a given text that has been made available in many cases. References have been added in some cases to other important articles or notes where different photos may have been published or further information on a text may have been supplied. The reader should realize that the long and tedious process of fitting fragments together and identifying them has at times meant the reordering of material, even after it has once been published in a preliminary fashion, because it has subsequently been recognized that certain pieces should be associated differently. An effort has been made here to list the material according to the present state of the question in this matter; this means that the sigla on some occasions may differ from what is given in a previous preliminary publication. The short Latin word *olim* ("formerly") has been used to indicate the change of sigla, where this is known.

The texts are listed here according to the numbered caves with their conventional sigla. The numbered caves designate only those in which written material has been discovered, not all the caves (e.g., in the Qumran area) where artifacts and evidence of habitation have been found.

I. QUMRAN

A. *Cave 1*

(1) *OT Texts*

1QIsa[a] Burrows, M. (ed.), *The Dead Sea Scrolls of St. Mark's Monastery* (New Haven: American Schools of Oriental Research), 1 (1950) pls. I-LIV (contains all 66 chs. of Isaiah with occasional lacunae with a few words missing at the bottom of some columns).

Cross, F. M. et al. (eds.), *Scrolls from Qumrân Cave I: The Great Isaiah Scroll, the Order of the Community, the* Pesher *to Habakkuk*. From photographs by John C. Trever (Jerusalem: Albright Institute of Archaeological Research and the Shrine of the Book, 1972), pp. [13]-[123]. (Black-and-white and colored photographs of cols. I-LIV of 1QIsa[a]; the black-and-white photographs are, however, not as good as those of the "first printing" of 1950.)

1QIsa[b] Sukenik, E. L., *'Oṣar ham-m[e]gillôt hag-g[e]nûzôt še-bîdê ha-'ûnîbersîṭāh ha-'ibrît* (Jerusalem: Bialik Foundation and the Hebrew University, [1954 (but the title-page incorrectly reads 1956)]), pls. 1-15. Two parts: Plates and Transcription. Modern Hebrew edition; the English version of it follows.

(DSSHU) Sukenik, E. L. (posthumously edited by N. Avigad and Y. Yadin), *The Dead Sea Scrolls of the Hebrew University* (Jerusalem: Hebrew University and Magnes Press, 1955). Two parts: Plates and Transcriptions. (See also 1Q*8* [DJD 1. 66-68])

Detailed Listing of Contents of 1QIsa[b]

1Q*8* 1:1-8	(DJD 1. 66; pl. XII)	Isa 7:22-8:1
DSSHU fr. 1	(pl. 1)	Isa 10:17-19
1Q*8* 2:1-9	(DJD 1. 66; pl. XII)	Isa 12:3-13:8
DSSHU fr. 2	(pl. 1)	Isa 13:16-19
1Q*8* 3:1-10	(DJD 1. 67; pl. XII)	Isa 15:3-16:2
DSSHU fr. 3	(pl. 1)	Isa 16:7-11
1Q*8* 4:1-10	(DJD 1. 67; pl. XII)	Isa 19:7-17
DSSHU fr. 4	(pl. 1)	Isa 19:20-20:1
1Q*8* 5:1-10	(DJD 1. 67; pl. XII)	Isa 22:11-18
DSSHU fr. 5	(pl. 1)	Isa 22:24-23:4

1Q*8* 6:1-15	(DJD 1. 68; pl. XII)	Isa 24:18-25:8
DSSHU fr. 6	(pl. 2)	Isa 26:1-5; 28:15-19
fr. 7	(pl. 2)	Isa 29:1-8
fr. 8	(pl. 2)	Isa 30:10-14
fr. 9	(pl. 2)	Isa 30:21-26
fr. 10	(pl. 2)	Isa 35:4-6
fr. 11	(pl. 2)	Isa 37:8-12
col. 1 + fr. 12	(pl. 3)	Isa 38:12-39:8; 40:2-3
col. 2	(pl. 4)	Isa 41:3-23
col. 3 + fr. 13	(pl. 5)	Isa 43:1-13, 23-27
col. 4	(pl. 6)	Isa 44:21-28; 45:1-13
col. 5	(pl. 7)	Isa 46:3-13; 47:1-14
col. 6	(pl. 8)	Isa 48:17-22; 49:1-15
col. 7	(pl. 9)	Isa 50:7-11; 51:1-10
col. 8	(pl. 10)	Isa 52:7-15; 53:1-12; 54:1-6
col. 9	(pl. 11)	Isa 55:2-13; 56:1-12; 57:1-4
col. 10	(pl. 12)	Isa 57:17-21; 58:1-14; 59:1-8
col. 11	(pl. 13)	Isa 59:20-21; 60:1-22; 61:1-2
col. 12	(pl. 14)	Isa 62:2-12; 63:1-19; 64:1, 6-8
col. 13	(pl. 15)	Isa 65:17-25; 66:1-24
1Q*8* fr. 7	(DJD 1. 68; pl. XII)	Isa ?

1QDan[a,b] Trever, J. C. "Completion of the Publication of Some Fragments from Qumran Cave I," *RQ* 5 (1964-66) 323-44 (it includes pls. I-VII, which belong to the texts transcribed in DJD 1. 150-55 [= 1Q*71-72*]) (1QDan[a] = Dan 1:10-17; 2:2-6; 1QDan[b] = Dan 3:22-30)

For other OT Texts found in DJD 1, see the detailed listing of 1Q*1-72* below.

(2) *Pesharim*

1QpHab — Burrows, M. (ed.), *The Dead Sea Scrolls of St. Mark's Monastery*, vol. 1, pls. LV-LXI (commentary on Hab 1:2-17; 2:1-20).

Cross, F. M. et al. (eds.), *Scrolls from Qumrân Cave I*, pp. [149]-[163] (Again, black-and-white and colored photographs of 1QpHab I-XIII)

(3) *Apocryphal and Sectarian Texts*

1QS — Burrows, M. (ed.), *The Dead Sea Scrolls of St. Mark's Monastery*, vol. 2, fasc. 2 ("The Manual of Discipline" [New Haven: American Schools of Oriental Research, 1951]), cols. I-XI.

Cross, F. M. et al. (eds.), *Scrolls from Qumrân Cave I*, pp. [125]-[147] (Again, black-and-white and colored photographs of 1QS I-XI)

1QapGen — Avigad, N. and Y. Yadin, *A Genesis Apocryphon: A Scroll from the Wilderness of Judaea. Description and Contents of the Scroll, Facsimiles, Transcriptions and Translation of Columns II, XIX-XXII* (Jerusalem: Magnes Press of the Hebrew University and Heikhal Ha-Sefer, 1956) (See also 1Q*20* [DJD 1. 86-87])

(A paraphrase, with inserts, of Gen 6:8-9; 9:2-3, 4, 20; Gen 10?; Gen 12:8-15:4 in Aramaic) [N.B. Fasc. 1 of vol. 2 of M. Burrows (ed.), *The Dead Sea Scrolls of St. Mark's Monastery* (see above), was reserved for this text originally; but it was published separately in Israel in 1956.])

1QM — Sukenik, E. L., *DSSHU*, pls. 16-34, 47 (lower); transcription, *dp* 1-19. (See also 1Q*33* [DJD 1. 135-36]) The War Scroll *(Milḥāmāh)*

1QH — Sukenik, E. L., *DSSHU*, pls. 35-47 (upper), 48-58; *dp* 1-18, frs. 1-66. (See also 1Q*35* [DJD 1.

136-38 = 1QH 7:27-8:13) The Thanksgiving Psalms (*Hôdāyôt*). Cf. *RB* 63 (1956) 64.

1QNoah 2, 1QPrs 2, 3 — Trever, J. C., "Completion of the Publication," *RQ* 5 (1964-66) 323-44 (+ pls. IV, VII)

1Q*1-72* — Barthélemy, D. and J. T. Milik, *Qumran Cave I* (DJD 1; Oxford: Clarendon, 1955)

Detailed Listing of 1Q*1-72* in DJD 1

(1) *OT Texts*

1Q*1*	1QGen	Gen 1:18-21; 3:11-14; 22:13-15; 23:17-19; 24: 22-24 + fragments
1Q*2*	1QExod	Exod 16:12-16; 19:24-20:1; 20:5-6; 20:25-21:1, 4-5 + fragments
1Q*3*	1QLev	Lev 11:10-11; 19:30-34; 20:20-24; 21:24-22:6; 23:4-8; Num 1:48-50; 36:7-8(?) + fragments (possibly Lev 27:30-31).
1Q*4*	1QDeut[a]	Deut 1:22-25; 4:47-49; 8:18-19; 8:19(?); 9:27-28; 11:27-30; 13:1-4, 4-6, 13-14; 14:21, 24-25; 16:4, 6-7 + fragments
1Q*5*	1QDeut[b]	Deut 1:9-13; 8:8-9; 9:10; 11:30-31; 15:14-15; 17:16; 21:8-9; 24:10-16; 25:13-18; 28:44-48; 29:9-11, 12-20; 30:19-31:6, 7-10, 12-13; 32: 17-21, 21-22, 22-29, 24-25; 33:12-17, 18-19, 21-23, 24 + fragments.
1Q*6*	1QJudg	Judg 6:20-22; 8:1(?); 9:1-4, 4-6, 28-31, 40-42, 40-43, 48-49 + fragments
1Q*7*	1QSam	1 Sam 18:17-18; 2 Sam 20:6-10; 21:16-18; 23: 9-12
1Q*8*	1QIsa[b]	Isa 7:22-8:1; 12:3-13:8; 15:3-16:2; 19:7-17; 22:11-18; 24:18-25:8
1Q*9*	1QEzek	Ezek 4:16-5:1
1Q*10*	1QPs[a]	Pss 86:5-8; 92:12-14; 94:16; 95:11-96:2; 119: 31-34, 43-48, 77-79 + fragments
1Q*11*	1QPs[b]	Pss 126:6; 127:1-5
1Q*12*	1QPs[c]	Ps 44:3-5, 4, 7, 9, 23-24, 25 + fragments
1Q*71*	1QDan[a]	Dan 1:10-17; 2:2-6 (DJD 1. 150-51)
1Q*72*	1QDan[b]	Dan 3:22-28, 27-30 (DJD 1. 151-52)

(2) *Phylacteries*

1Q*13*	1QPhyl	= Deut 5:23-27; 10:17-18; 10:21-11:1, 8-11, 12; Exod 13:2-3, 7-9 + fragments

(3) *Pesharim*

1Q*14*	1QpMic	Pesher on Mic 1:2-5, 5-7, 8-9; 4:13(?); 6:14-16; 7:6(?), 8-9(?), 17
1Q*15*	1QpZeph	Pesher on Zeph 1:18-2:2
1Q*16*	1QpPs	Pesher on Ps 57:1, 4; 68:12-13, 26-27, 30-31 + fragments

(4) *Apocryphal Texts*

1Q*17-18*	1QJub^{a,b}	= Jub 27:19-21; 35:8-10 + fragments [36:12(?)]
1Q*19*, *19* bis	1QNoah	Book of Noah [related to 1 Enoch 8:4-9:4; 106: 9-10] (DJD 1. 84-86, 152)
1Q*20*	1QapGen	*olim* "Apocalypse of Lamech"
1Q*21*	1QTLevi ar	= Testament of Levi 8:11(?), older form of Bodleian CTLevi ar
1Q*22*	1QDM	"Dires de Moïse" or Dibrê Mōšeh (Sayings of Moses)
1Q*23-24*	1QHenGiants	"Book of the Giants" (see J. T. Milik, "Turfan et Qumran," *Tradition und Glaube: Das frühe Christentum in seiner Umwelt: Festgabe für K. G. Kuhn* [Göttingen: Vandenhoeck & Ruprecht, 1971] 120-21) (*olim* "une prophétie apocryphe")
1Q*25*		"Une prophétie apocryphe (?)" (Hebrew)
1Q*26*		A Wisdom apocryphon (genre of Testaments and Instructions) (Hebrew)
1Q*27*	1QMyst	Book of the Mysteries (Hebrew; cf. *RB* 63 [1956] 61)

(5) *Sectarian Texts*

1Q*28*		Appendices to 1QS:
1Q*28a*	1QSa	"Règle de la Congrégation" (Rule for all the Congregation of Israel in the End of Days) (Hebrew)
1Q*28b*	1QSb	Collection of Benedictions (Hebrew)
1Q*29*		Liturgy of Three Tongues of Fire(?) (Hebrew); cf. *RB* 63 (1956) 64
1Q*30-31*		Liturgical Texts (?) (Hebrew)
1Q*32*	1QJN ar	Description of the New Jerusalem(?) (Aramaic)
1Q*33*	1QM frs. 1-2	Fragments belonging to War Scroll (1QM)
1Q*34*		Liturgical Prayers (Hebrew)
1Q*34* bis		Liturgical Prayers (DJD 1. 152-55)
1Q*35*	1QH frs.	Fragments belonging to *Hôdāyôt* (1QH)
1Q*36*		Fragments of a collection of hymns (Hebrew)
1Q*37-40*		Hymnic compositions (?) (Hebrew)

1Q*41-62*	Unidentified, tiny Hebrew fragments
1Q*63-67*	Unidentified, tiny Aramaic fragments
1Q*68*	Unclassified Aramaic fragments
1Q*69*	Unclassified Hebrew fragments
1Q*70*	Tiny papyrus fragments
1Q*70* bis	Papyrus fragment (DJD 1. 155)

B. *Caves 2-3, 5-10* ("Minor Caves")

2Q*1-33*
3Q*1-15*
5Q*1-25*
6Q*1-31*
7Q*1-19*
8Q*1-5*
9Q*1* (pap)
10Q*1* (ostr)

Baillet, M., J. T. Milik, and R. de Vaux, *Les 'Petites Grottes' de Qumrân: Exploration de la falaise, les grottes 2Q, 3Q, 5Q, 6Q, 7Q à 10Q, le rouleau de cuivre* (DJD 3; Oxford: Clarendon, 1962) Two parts: 1. Texte; 2. Planches

3Q*15*

The Copper Plaque or "the Copper Rolls"

Allegro, J. M., *The Treasure of the Copper Scroll* (Garden City, NY: Doubleday, 1960) (See DJD 3. 299; *RB* 68 [1961] 146-47)

The official publication is by J. T. Milik, "Le rouleau de cuivre provenant de la grotte 3Q (3Q15)," DJD 3. 199-302

Detailed Listing of 2Q*1-33* in DJD 3

(1) *OT Texts*

2Q*1*	2QGen	Gen 19:27-28; 36:6, 35-37
2Q*2*	2QExod[a]	Exod 1:11-14; 7:1-4; 9:27-29; 11:3-7; 12:32-41; 21:18-20(?); 26:11-13; 30:21(?), 23-25; 32:32-34
2Q*3*	2QExod[b]	Exod 4:31; 12:26-27(?); 18:21-22; 21:37-22:2, 15-19; 27:17-19; 31:16-17; 19:9; 34:10 + fragments
2Q*4*	2QExod[c]	Exod 5:3-5
2Q*5*	2QpaleoLev	Lev 11:22-29
2Q*6*	2QNum[a]	Num 3:38-41; 3:51-4:3
2Q*7*	2QNum[b]	Num 33:47-53
2Q*8*	2QNum[c]	Num 7:88
2Q*9*	2QNum[d(?)]	Num 18:8-9 (possibly belongs to 2Q*7*; possibly is Lev 23:1-3)
2Q*10*	2QDeut[a]	Deut 1:7-9
2Q*11*	2QDeut[b]	Deut 17:12-15
2Q*12*	2QDeut[c]	Deut 10:8-12
2Q*13*	2QJer	Jer 42:14; 43:8-11; 44:1-3, 12-14; 46:27-47:7; 48:7, 25-39, 43-45; 49:10 + fragments (some doubtfully identified: 13:22; 32:24-25; 48:2-4, 41-42)

2Q*14*	2QPs	Ps 103:2-11; 104:6-11
2Q*15*	2QJob	Job 33:28-30
2Q*16*	2QRuth[a]	Ruth 2:13-14, 14-19, 19-22; 2:22-3:3, 4-8; 4:3-4
2Q*17*	2QRuth[b]	Ruth 3:13-18
2Q*18*	2QSir	Sir 6:14-15 (? *or* 1:19-20); 6:20-31

(2) *Apocryphal Texts*

2Q*19*	2QJub[a]	Jub 23:7-8 (cf. Gen 25:9, 7-8)
2Q*20*	2QJub[b]	Jub 46:1-3 (cf. Exod 1:7; Gen 50:26, 22) + frs. of uncertain relation
2Q*21*	2QapMoses	Apocryphon of Moses (?)
2Q*22*	2QapDavid	Apocryphon of David (?)
2Q*23*	2QapProph	Prophetic Apocryphon
2Q*24*	2QJN ar	Description of the New Jerusalem

(3) *Sectarian Juridical and Liturgical Texts*

2Q*25*	2Q?	A Juridical Document
2Q*26*	2Q? ar	A Ritual Fragment (?)
2Q*27-33*	2Q?	Tiny, ill-defined fragments

Detailed Listing of 3Q*1-15* in DJD 3

(1) *OT Texts*

3Q*1*	3QEzek	Ezek 16:31-33
3Q*2*	3QPs	Ps 2:6-7
3Q*3*	3QLam	Lam 1:10-12; 3:53-62

(2) *Pesharim*

3Q*4*	3QpIsa	Pesher on Isa 1:1

(3) *Apocryphal Texts*

3Q*5*	3QJub (*olim* 3QapProph)	Originally called an apocryphal prophecy, it is now considered to be a fragment of *Jubilees*, probably = 23:12-13; cf. R. Deichgräber, "Fragmente einer Jubiläen-Handschrift aus Höhle 3 von Qumran," *RQ* 5 (1964-65) 415-22; but also A. Rofé, "Further Manuscript Fragments of the Jubilees in the Third Cave of Qumran," *Tarbiẓ* 34 (1965) 333-36
3Q*6*	3QHymn	Hymn of Praise

3Q*7*	3Q?	Text about an Angel of the Presence
3Q*8*	3Q?	Text about an Angel of Peace
3Q*9*	3Q?	Sectarian text(?)
3Q*10-11*	3Q?	Tiny, ill-defined fragments (Hebrew)
3Q*12-13*	3Q? ar	Tiny, ill-defined fragments (Aramaic)
3Q*14*	3Q?	Isolated fragments
3Q*15*	3QTreasure	Copper plaque mentioning Buried Treasure(s); see section 11 below

Detailed Listing of 5Q*1-25* in DJD 3

(1) *OT Texts*

5Q*1*	5QDeut	Deut 7:15-24; 8:5-9:2
5Q*2*	5QKgs	1 Kgs 1:1, 16-17, 27-37
5Q*3*	5QIsa	Isa 40:16, 18-19
5Q*4*	5QAmos	Amos 1:3-5
5Q*5*	5QPs	Ps 119:99-101, 104, 113-20, 138-42
5Q*6*	5QLam[a]	Lam 4:5-8, 11-15, 15-16, 19-20; 4:20-5:3, 4-12, 12-13, 16-17 + fragments
5Q*7*	5QLam[b]	Lam 4:17-20
5Q*8*	5QPhyl	"Vu leur état désespéré, je les ai laissées non déroulées."

(2) *Apocryphal Texts*

5Q*9*	5QToponyms	A text with toponyms
5Q*10*	5QapMal	Apocryphon of Malachi (? [cites Mal 1:13-14])
5Q*11*	5QS	Serek hay-Yaḥad (= 1QS 2:4-7, 11-14[?])
5Q*12*	5QD	Damascus Document (= CD 9:7-10)
5Q*13*	5QRègle	Fragments related to 1QS, but not identical with it or with CD
5Q*14*	5QCurses	Liturgical Composition with Curses
5Q*15*	5QJN ar	Description of the New Jerusalem (includes readings from 4QJN and 11QJN)
5Q*16-24*	5Q?	Tiny, ill-defined fragments
5Q*25*	5Q?	Unclassified fragments

Detailed Listing of 6Q*1-31* in DJD 3

(1) *OT Texts*

6Q*1*	6QpaleoGen	Gen 6:13-21
6Q*2*	6QpaleoLev	Lev 8:12-13

6Q*3*	6QDeut	Possibly Deut 26:19
6Q*4*	6QKgs	1 Kgs 3:12-14; 12:28-31; 22:28-31; 2 Kgs 5:26; 6:32; 7:8-10; 7:20-8:5; 9:1-2; 10:19-21 + many isolated fragments
6Q*5*	6QPs	Ps 78:36-37 (?)
6Q*6*	6QCant	Cant 1:1-6, 6-7
6Q*7*	6QDan	Dan 8:20-21(?); 10:8-16; 11:33-36, 38; 8:16-17(?)

(2) *Apocryphal Texts*

6Q*8*	6QapGen ar	Genesis Apocryphon (related to 1QapGen ?) (Aramaic)
6Q*9*	6QapSam/Kgs	Samuel-Kings Apocryphon (Hebrew)
pap6Q*10*	6QProph	Prophetic Text (Hebrew)
6Q*11*	6QAllegory	Allegory of the Vine (?) (Hebrew)
6Q*12*	6QapProph	Prophetic Apocryphon (Hebrew)
6Q*13*	6QPriestProph	Priestly Prophecy (?) (Hebrew text related to Ezra-Nehemiah ?)
6Q*14*	6QApoc ar	Apocalyptic Text (Aramaic)

(3) *Sectarian Texts*

6Q*15*	6QD	Damascus Document (= CD 4:19-21; 5:13-14; 5:18-6:2; 6:20-7:1 + a fragment that is not found in CD)
pap6Q*16*	6QBen	Blessings or Benedictions
6Q*17*	6QCal	Calendar fragments
pap6Q*18*	6QHymn	Hymnic Composition

(4) *Tiny Ill-Defined Fragments*

6Q*19*	6QGen(?) ar	Text Related to Genesis (10:6, 20) (?) (Aramaic)
6Q*20*	6QDeut(?)	Text Related to Deuteronomy (11:10) (?)
6Q*21*	6QfrProph	Prophetic Fragment (?)
6Q*22*	6Q? hebr	Hebrew Text
6Q*23*	6Q? ar	Aramaic Text
6Q*24-31*	6Q?	

Detailed Listing of 7Q*1-19* in DJD 3

(1) *OT Texts*

7Q*1*	7QExod gr	Exod 28:4-7
7Q*2*	7QEpJer gr	Vss. 43-44

(2) *Biblical Texts (?)* [All in Greek]. See section 10/VII below.

7Q*3*	
7Q*4*	
7Q*5*	
7Q*6*	
7Q*7*	
7Q*8*	
7Q*9*	
7Q*10*	
7Q*11*	
7Q*12*	
7Q*13-18*	Very tiny papyrus fragments
7Q*19*	Imprints of papyrus with writing on plaster fragments

Detailed Listing of 8Q*1-5* in DJD 3

(1) *OT Texts*

8Q*1*	8QGen	Gen 17:12-19
8Q*2*	8QPs	Ps 17:5-9, 14; 18:6-9 (= 2 Sam 22:6-9); 18:10-13 (= 2 Sam 22:10-13)
8Q*3*	8QPhyl	Phylactery
8Q*4*	8QMez	Mezuzah (Deut 10:12-11:21)

(2) *Liturgical Text*

8Q*5*	8QHymn	Hymnic Text

N.B. From 9Q has come only one papyrus fragment (unidentified), and from 10Q has come only one piece of inscribed pottery (ostracon ?).

C. *Cave 4*

(1) *OT Texts*

4QExod[a] Cross, F. M., *ALQ*, 184-85 (transliteration of fr. 1 only, but see the plate opposite p. 141) (= Exod 1:1-5)

4QExod[c] Cross, F. M., "The Song of the Sea and Canaanite Myth," *JTC* 5 (1968) 1-25, esp. pp. 13-16 (= Exod 15:1b-18)

4QExod[f] Cross, F. M., *SWDS*, 14, 23 (= Exod 40:8-27)

4QpaleoExod[m] Skehan, P. W., "Exodus in the Samaritan Recension from Qumran," *JBL* 74 (1955) 182-87; see the photograph in *BA* 28 (1965) 98; *SWDS*, 16, 26 (= Exod 6:25-7:19)

4QDeut[n] Cross, F. M., *SWDS*, 20, 31-32. The "All Souls Deuteronomy Scroll" (On page 20 it bears the siglum 4QDeut[m]! This is incorrect, as F. M. Cross informs me); cf. H. Stegemann, "Weitere Stücke von 4QpPsalm 37, von 4Q Patriarchal Blessings, und Hinweis auf eine unedierte Handschrift aus Höhle 4Q mit Exzerpten aus dem Deuteronomium," *RQ* 6 (1967-69) 193-227, esp. pp. 217-27 (= Deut 5:1-6:1; 8:5-10)

4QDeut[q] Skehan, P. W., "A Fragment of the 'Song of Moses' (Deut 32) from Qumran," *BASOR* 136 (1954) 12-15; "The Qumran Manuscripts and Textual Criticism," *Volume du congrès, Strasbourg 1956* (VTSup 4; Leiden: Brill, 1957) 148-60, esp. p. 150 n. 1 (= Deut 32:37-43)

4QSam[a] Cross, F. M., "A New Qumran Biblical Fragment Related to the Original Hebrew Underlying the Septuagint," *BASOR* 132 (1953) 15-26; cf. *SWDS*, 14, 24-25; *ALQ*, 188-89 n. 40a, p. 191 n. 45; P. W. Skehan, *BA* 28 (1965) (= 1 Sam 1:22b-2:6; 2:16-25)

4QSam[b] Cross, F. M., "The Oldest Manuscripts from Qumran," *JBL* 74 (1955) 147-72, esp. pp. 165-72 (= 1 Sam 16:1-11; 19:10-17; 21:3-10; 23:9-17)

4QSam[a,b,c] Variants	(Cross, F. M.), "Textual Notes" on 1-2 Samuel in *The New American Bible* (Paterson, NJ: St. Anthony Guild, 1970) 342-51 (This edition must be consulted because the textual notes are not always reproduced in other printings of the *NAB*.)
4QIsa[a]	Muilenburg, J., "Fragments of Another Qumran Isaiah Scroll," *BASOR* 135 (1954) 28-32 (= Isa 12:5-13:6; 22:13d-23:6a)
4QJer[b]	Cross, F. M., *ALQ*, 187 (transliteration only of Jer 10:4, 9, 11)
4QJer[a,b]	Janzen, J. G., *Studies in the Text of Jeremiah* (Harvard Semitic Monographs, 6: Cambridge: Harvard University, 1973) 173-84 (Appendix D: "Hebrew Texts of Jeremiah from Qumran") (Jer[a] = Jer 7:29-9:2; 9:7-14; 10:9-14; 11:3-6; 12:3-6; 12:17-13:7; 14:4-7; 15:1-2; 17:8-26; 18:15-19:1; 22:4-16. Jer[b] = Jer 9:22-10:18; 43:3-9; 50:4-6)
4QXII[?]	Testuz, M., "Deux fragments inédits des manuscrits de la Mer Morte," *Semitica* 5 (1955) 37-38 (= Hos 13:15b-14:1a, 3-6)
4QPs[b]	Skehan, P. W., "A Psalm Manuscript from Qumran (4QPs[b])," *CBQ* 26 (1964) 313-22; cf. *SWDS*, 20, 30-31 (= Ps 91:5-8, 12-15; 92:4-8, 13-15; 94:1-4, 8-9, 10-14, 17-18, 21-22; 99:5-6; 100:1-2; 102:10-17, 18-25; 102:26-103:3, 4-6, 9-11, 20-21; 112:4-5; 116:17-19; 118:1-3, 6-11, 18-20, 23-26)
4QPs[f]	Starcky, J., "Psaumes apocryphes de la grotte 4 de Qumrân (4QPs[f] VII-X)," *RB* 73 (1966) 353-71 (= Ps 109:23-31)
4QPs[q]	Milik, J. T., "Deux documents inédits du Désert de Juda," *Bib* 38 (1957) 245-68, esp. pp. 245-55 (+ pl. I) (= Ps 31:24-25 + 33:1-18; 35:4-20)

4QPs89 — Milik, J. T., "Fragment d'une source du psautier (4Q Ps 89) et fragments des Jubilés, du Document de Damas, d'une phylactère dans la grotte 4 de Qumran," *RB* 73 (1966) 94-106, esp. pp. 95-98 (+ pl. I) (= Ps 89:20-31) (4Q*236*)

4QPs^{a-q} — Sanders, J. A., *DSPS*, 143-55 (Appendix II: "Pre-Masoretic Psalter Texts"--a catalogue and an index of all the Qumran, Masada, and Ḥever psalm-texts, in which one can quickly find where a fragment of a given psalm may be found)

4QXII^{d} — Wolff, H. W., *Hosea: A Commentary on the Book of the Prophet Hosea* (tr. G. Stansell; Hermeneia; Philadelphia: Fortress, 1974) v (photograph of 4QXII^{d} = Hos 1:7-2:5)

4QQoh^{a} — Muilenburg, J., "A Qoheleth Scroll from Qumran," *BASOR* 135 (1954) 20-28 (= Qoh 5:13-17; 6:3-8; 7:7-9)

4QLXXLev^{a} — Skehan, P. W., "The Qumran Manuscripts and Textual Criticism," *Volume du Congrès, Strasbourg 1956* (VTSup 4; Leiden: Brill, 1957) 148-60, esp. pp. 159-60; cf. *SWDS*, 15, 25 (= Lev 26:2-16)

4QLXXNum — Skehan, P. W., "The Qumran Manuscripts," VTSup 4, 155-56; cf. "The Biblical Scrolls from Qumran and the Text of the Old Testament," *BA* 28 (1965) 87-100, esp. pp. 90-91 (with photograph) (= Num 3:40-42; 4:6-9)

4QTob ar^{a-d}
4QTob hebr^{a} — Milik, J. T., "La patrie de Tobie," *RB* 73 (1966) 522-30, esp. p. 522 n. 3 (where Milik gives the list of passages in Tobit which are present in 4QTob ar^{a-d} and 4QTob hebr^{a}, but none of the text)

(2) *Phylacteries*

4QPhyl^{a-d} — Kuhn, K. G., *Phylakterien aus Höhle 4 von Qumran* (Abhandlungen der Heidelberger Akademie der

Wissenschaften, Philos.-hist. Kl., 1957/1; Heidelberg: C. Winter, 1957)

4QPhyl I — Milik, J. T., "Fragment d'une source," *RB* 73 (1966) 105-6 (+ pl. IIb)

(3) *Pesharim*

4Q*158-186* — Allegro, J. M. (with the collaboration of A. A. Anderson), *Qumrân Cave 4: I (4Q158-4Q186)* (DJD 5; Oxford: Clarendon, 1968) (This publication must be used with caution: some fragments have not been properly identified or joined; many readings are questionable; the numbering of plates is confusing; the secondary literature on the fifteen texts in it that were previously published in partial or preliminary form has normally been neglected. Essential for further work on these texts are the following: J. Strugnell, "Notes en marge du volume V des 'Discoveries in the Judaean Desert of Jordan,'" *RQ* 7 [1969-71] 163-276; J. A. Fitzmyer, "A Bibliographical Aid to the Study of Qumrân Cave IV Texts 158-86," *CBQ* 31 [1969] 59-71. The preliminary publications are listed below; for the biblical passages on which these pesharim comment, see the detailed listing further on, p. 33). Criticism of this volume has been severe: "Überhaupt ist DJD V die schlechteste und unzuverlässigste Q-Edition, die seit dem Beginn der Funde dem Leser zugemutet wurde" (K. Müller, "Die Handschriften" [see section 5 below] 310). "'R' habet italicum liber hic, habet atque Pelasgum, Necnon hebraeum, praetereaque nihil!" (J. Strugnell, *RQ* 7 [1969-71] 276; cf. *America* 123 [26 Sept. 1970] 207).

4QpIsa[a] — Allegro, J. M., "Further Messianic References in Qumran Literature," *JBL* 75 (1956) 174-87, esp. pp. 177-82 (Document III, 4 frs., pls. II-III); DJD 5. 11-15; pls. IV-V (4Q*161*)

4QpIsa[b] Allegro, J. M., "More Isaiah Commentaries from Qumran's Fourth Cave," *JBL* 77 (1958) 215-21, esp. pp. 215-18 (+ pl. 1); DJD 5. 15-17; pl. VI (4Q*162*)

pap4QpIsa[c] Allegro, J. M., "More Isaiah Commentaries," *JBL* 77 (1958) 218-20 (+ pl. 2); DJD 5. 17-27; pls. VII-VIII (4Q*163*)

4QpIsa[d] Allegro, J. M., "More Isaiah Commentaries," *JBL* 77 (1958) 220-21 (+ pl. 3); DJD 5. 27-28; pl. IX (3 frs., upper) (4Q*164*)

4QpIsa[e] Allegro, J. M., DJD 5. 28-30; pl. IX (10 frs., lower) (4Q*165*)

4QpHos[a] (*olim* 4QpHos[b]) Allegro, J. M., "A Recently Discovered Fragment of a Commentary on Hosea from Qumran's Fourth Cave," *JBL* 78 (1959) 142-47; DJD 5. 31-32; pl. X (4Q*166*)

4QpHos[b] (*olim* 4QpHos[a]) Allegro, J. M., "Further Light on the History of the Qumran Sect," *JBL* 75 (1956) 89-95, esp. p. 93 (+ pl. 2); DJD 5. 32-36; pls. X-XI (4Q*167*)

4QpMic(?) Allegro, J. M., DJD 5. 36; pl. XII (4 frs., upper left) (4Q*168*)

4QpNah Allegro, J. M., "Further Light," *JBL* 75 (1956) 90-93 (+ pl. 1); "More Unpublished Pieces of a Qumran Commentary on Nahum (4QpNah)," *JSS* 7 (1962) 304-8; cf. *SWDS*, 17, 26-27; DJD 5. 37-42; pls. XII (upper right and lower fragments), XII, XIV (upper fragments) (4Q*169*)

4QpZeph Allegro, J. M., DJD 5. 42; pl. XIV (center) (4Q*170*)

4QpPs[a] (*olim* 4QpPs 37) Allegro, J. M., "A Newly Discovered Fragment of a Commentary on Psalm XXXVII," *PEQ* 86 (1954) 69-75; "Further Light," *JBL* 75 (1956) 94-95 (+ pl. 4); *The People of the Dead Sea Scrolls in Text and Pictures* (Garden City: Doubleday, 1958) 86-87 (pls. 48, 50); DJD 5. 42-51; pls. XIV (lower frs.), XV, XVI, XVII (4Q*171*)

Stegemann, H., "Der Pešer Psalm 37 aus Höhle 4 von Qumran (4Q p Ps 37)," *RQ* 4 (1963-64) 235-70; "Weitere Stücke von 4QpPsalm 37," *RQ* 6 (1967-69) 193-210.

4QpPs[b] — Allegro, J. M., DJD 5. 51-53; pl. XVIII (5 frs., center) (4Q*173*)

4QpUnid — Allegro, J. M., DJD 5. 50-51; pl. XVIII (14 frs., upper) (4Q*172*) [an unidentified pesher]

(4) *Apocryphal and Sectarian Texts*

4QBibParaph — Allegro, J. M., DJD 5. 1-6; pl. I (4Q*158*)

4QOrd — Allegro, J. M., "An Unpublished Fragment of Essene Halakah (4Q Ordinances)," *JSS* 6 (1961) 71-73; DJD 5. 6-9; pl. II (4Q*159*)

4QVisSamuel — Allegro, J. M., DJD 5. 9-11; pl. III (4Q*160*)

4QFlor (*or* 4QEschMidr) — Allegro, J. M., "Further Messianic References," *JBL* 75 (1956) 176-77 (Document II, pl. 1); "Fragments of a Qumran Scroll of Eschatological Midrašîm," *JBL* 77 (1958) 350-54; DJD 5. 53-57; pls. XIX-XX (4Q*174*)

4QTestim — Allegro, J. M., "Further Messianic References," *JBL* 75 (1956) 182-87 (Document IV, pl. 4); DJD 5. 57-60; pl. XXI (4Q*175*) Contains a proto-Samaritan text of Exod 20:21 (conflating Deut 5:28-29 and 18:18-19 [see P. W. Skehan, *CBQ* 19 (1957) 435-40]); Num 24:15-17; Deut 33:8-11; Josh 6:26 and PssJosh (see below 4QPssJosh)

4QTanḥumim — Allegro, J. M., DJD 5. 60-67; pls. XXII-XXIII (4Q*176*); contains Ps 79:2-3; Isa 40:1-5; 41:8-9; 49:7, 13-17; 43:4-6; 51:22-23; 52:1-3; 54:4-10; 52:1-2; Zech 13:9.

4QCatena[a] — Allegro, J. M., DJD 5. 67-74; pls. XXIV-XXV (upper) (4Q*177*) (apocalyptic view of victory of the community)

4Q? — Allegro, J. M., DJD 5. 74-75; pl. XXV (13 frs., lower) (4Q*178*)

4QapLam — Allegro, J. M., DJD 5. 75-77; pls. XXVI (upper) (4Q*179*)
(N.B. This is not a copy of canonical Lamentations)

4QAgesCreat — Allegro, J. M., "Some Unpublished Fragments of Pseudepigraphical Literature from Qumran's Fourth Cave," *ALUOS* 4 (1962-63) 3-5; DJD 5. 77-80; pls. XXVII (5 frs., upper), XVIII (3 frs., lower) (4Q*180-81*) Cf. J. T. Milik, "Milkî-ṣedeq et Milkî-rešaʿ dans les anciens écrits juifs et chrétiens," *JJS* 23 (1972) 95-144, esp. pp. 109-26.

4QCatena[b] — Allegro, J. M., DJD 5. 80-81; pls. XXVII (2 frs., lower) (4Q*182*)

4Q? — Allegro, J. M., DJD 5. 81-82; pl. XXVI (3 frs., lower) (4Q*183*)

4QWiles — Allegro, J. M., "The Wiles of the Wicked Woman: A Sapiential Work from Qumran's Fourth Cave," *PEQ* 96 (1964) 53-55; DJD 5. 82-85; pl. XXVIII (4Q*184*)

4Q? — Allegro, J. M., DJD 5. 85-87; pls. XXIX-XXX (4Q*185*)

4QCryptic — Allegro, J. M., "An Astrological Cryptic Document from Qumran," *JSS* 9 (1964) 291-94; DJD 5. 88-91; pl. XXXI (4Q*186*) (Possibly related to Enoch literature; see J. T. Milik, *HTR* 64 [1971] 366)

4QPBless (*olim* 4QpGen 49) — Allegro, J. M., "Further Messianic References," *JBL* 75 (1956) 174-76 (Document I, pl. 1) (Contains Gen 49:10; omitted from DJD 5; see J. A. Fitzmyer, *CBQ* 31 [1969] 71; cf. H. Stegemann, "Der Pešer Psalm 37," *RQ* 4 [1963-64] 211-17)

4QM[a-c] — Hunzinger, C.-H., "Fragmente einer älteren Fassung des Buches Milḥamā aus Höhle 4 von Qumrān," *ZAW* 69 (1957) 131-51; cf. *SWDS*, 18, 29 (= 1QM 14:3-16+)

pap4QM[e-f] — Baillet, M., "Débris de textes sur papyrus de la Grotte 4 de Qumran (Pl. XIV-XV)," *RB* 71 (1964) 353-71, esp. pp. 356-59, 365-71 (+ pl. XV);

	pap4QM^{e} = 1QM 1:11-14; 1QM 2:3-3:2; 10:16?; "Les manuscrits de la règle de la guerre de la grotte 4 de Qumran," *RB* 79 (1972) 217-26 (see esp. p. 225 for a list of 4QM^{a-f} frs. and their relation to 1QM; cf. J. T. Milik, "Milkî-ṣedeq et Milkî-rešaʿ," *JJS* 23 [1972] 140).
pap4QPrLit^{b}	Baillet, M., "Débris de textes," *RB* 71 (1964) 354-55, 360-65; "Psaumes, hymnes, cantiques et prières dans les manuscrits de Qumrân," *Le psautier: Ses origines. Ses problèmes littéraires. Son influence: Etudes présentées aux XIIe Journées Bibliques (29-31 août 1960)* (Orientalia et biblica lovaniensia, 4: Louvain: Publications universitaires, 1962) 389-405
4QPsDan ar^{a-c}	Milik, J. T., "'Prière de Nabonide' et autres écrits d'un cycle de Daniel, fragments de Qumrân 4," *RB* 63 (1956) 407-15, esp. pp. 411-15
4QPsDan A^{a}	Milik, J. T., Public Lecture at Harvard University, December 1972 (cf. J. A. Fitzmyer, "The Contribution of Qumran Aramaic to the Study of the New Testament," *NTS* 20 [1973-74] 382-407, esp. pp. 391-94) (4Q*243*)
4QPrNab (*or* 4QṣNab)	Milik, J. T., "'Prière de Nabonide,'" *RB* 63 (1956) 407-11
4QJub^{f}	Milik, J. T., "Fragment d'une source," *RB* 73 (1966) 104 (+ pl. IIa) (4Q*221* = Jub 21:22-24) [on 4QJub^{e}, see DJD 3. 226]
4QTLevi ar^{a} (*olim* 4QTLevi ar^{b})	Milik, J. T., "Le Testament de Lévi en araméen: Fragment de la grotte 4 de Qumrân," *RB* 62 (1955) 398-406; cf. *SWDS*, 16, 25-26 (related to CTLevi ar, Bodleian)
4QʿAmram^{b-e}	Milik, J. T., "4Q Visions de ʿAmram et une citation d'Origène," *RB* 79 (1972) 77-97, esp. pp. 78-92 (+ pl. I [= 4QʿAmram^{b}]); cf. J. A. Fitzmyer, *ESBNT*, 101-4
4QTQahat	Milik, J. T., "4Q Visions de ʿAmram," *RB* 79 (1972) 97

4QHenAstr[a-d] Milik, J. T., "Problèmes de la littérature hénochique à la lumière des fragments araméens de Qumrân," *HTR* 64 (1971) 333-78
(N.B. In the 4Q Enoch material beware of many changes of sigla. I cannot guarantee that I have sorted them all out properly; we shall have to await a long-announced publication of the Enoch literature from 4Q by J. T. Milik (in collaboration with M. Black [see the latter's article, "The Fragments of the Aramaic Enoch from Qumran," *La littérature juive entre Tenach et Mischna: Quelques problèmes* (RechBib 9; ed. W. C. van Unnik; Leiden: Brill, 1974) 15-28]).
(4QHen[a] = 1 Enoch ?; 4QHen[b] = ?; 4QHen[c] = 1 Enoch 30:1-32:1; 35:1-36:4; 4QHen[d] = 1 Enoch ?; 4QHen[e] = 1 Enoch 31:2-32:3; 4QHenAstr[b] = 1 Enoch 77:3)

4QHen[c,e] (*olim* 4QHen[b,d]) Milik, J. T., "Hénoch au pays des aromates (ch. xxvii à xxxii): Fragments araméens de la grotte 4 de Qumran," *RB* 65 (1958) 70-77
Milik, J. T., "Problèmes de la littérature hénochique," *HTR* 64 (1971) 333-78 (passim)

4QHenGiants[a-f] Milik, J. T., "Turfan et Qumran: Livre des Géants juif et manichéen," *Tradition und Glaube: Das frühe Christentum in seiner Umwelt: Festgabe für Karl Georg Kuhn zum 65. Geburtstag* (eds. G. Jeremias et al.; Göttingen: Vandenhoeck & Ruprecht, 1971) 117-27 (+ pl. I)

4QD[a] Milik, J. T., "Fragment d'une source," *RB* 73 (1966) 105 (+ pl. III) (A part of the Damascus Document that is not in CD, but is found in three other copies of 4QD. Milik here calls it 4Q*226*, but in thc following entry it is found listed as 4Q*266* [typographical error or change of siglum?]. It contains halakah related to Leviticus 13, 15). See J. T. Milik, *Ten Years*, 38-39; DJD 3. 181, 226.

4QD[a,e] Milik, J. T., "Milkî-ṣedeq et Milkî-reša'," *JJS* 23 (1972) 135-36 (4Q*266*, 4Q*270*)

4QS Variants	Milik, J. T., Review of P. Wernberg-Møller, *The Manual of Discipline Translated and Annotated* (Leiden: Brill, 1957), *RB* 67 (1960) 410-16, esp. pp. 412-16 (a list of the most significant variants in 4QS[a-j] texts from that of 1QS)
4QHalakah[a]	Milik, J. T., "Addenda à 3*Q15*," DJD 3. 299-302, esp. p. 300
4QṬeharot B	Milik, J. T., "Milkî-ṣedeq et Milkî-rešaʿ," *JJS* 23 (1972) 129-30 (4*Q275*)
4QṬeharot D	Milik, J. T., "Milkî-ṣedeq et Milkî-rešaʿ," *JJS* 23 (1972) 126-29 (+ pl. I)
4QBer[a,b]	Milik, J. T., "Milkî-ṣedeq et Milkî-rešaʿ," *JJS* 23 (1972) 130-35 (+ pl. II)
4QPssJosh	Spijkerman, P. A., "Chronique du Musée de la Flagellation," *SBFLA* 12 (1961-62) 323-33, esp. p. 325 (photograph); cf. 4QTestim
4QMess ar	Starcky, J., "Un texte messianique araméen de la grotte 4 de Qumrân," *Ecole des langues orientales anciennes de l'Institut Catholique de Paris: Mémorial du cinquantenaire 1914-1964* (Travaux de l'Institut Catholique de Paris, 10; Paris: Bloud et Gay, 1964) 51-66 (misnamed; it is not "messianic"; see J. A. Fitzmyer, "The Aramaic 'Elect of God' Text from Qumran Cave IV," *CBQ* 27 [1965] 348-72)
4QPsAp[a-c]	Starcky, J., "Psaumes apocryphes," *RB* 73 (1966) 353-71
4QJN	(Cf. J. Starcky, *RB* 63 [1956] 66; J. T. Milik on 5*Q15* [= 5QJN] in DJD 3. 184-93)
4QŠirŠabb (*olim* 4QSl 39-40)	Strugnell, J., "The Angelic Liturgy at Qumrân--4Q Serek Šîrôt ʿÔlat Haššabbāt," *Congress Volume, Oxford, 1959* (VTSup 7; Leiden: Brill, 1960) 318-45
4QTestuz ar	Testuz, M., "Deux fragments," *Semitica* 5 (1955) 38 (a text possibly related to the Enoch literature ["precious tablets," but beware of the plates, which are printed upside down with labels confused])

Detailed Listing of 4Q*158-186* in DJD 5

(A) *Pesharim*

4Q*161*	4QpIsa[a]	Commentary on Isa 10:20-21, 22, 24-27, 28-32, 33-34; 11:1-5
4Q*162*	4QpIsa[b]	Commentary on Isa 5:5-6, 11-14, 24-25, 29-30; 6:9(?)
4Q*163*	4QpIsa[c]	Commentary on Isa 8:7, 8, 9(?); 9:11(?), 14-20; 10:12, 13, 19(?), 20-24; 14:8, 26-30; 19: 9-12; 29:10-11, 15-16, 19-23; Zech 11:11; Isa 30:1-5, 15-18; Hos 6:9; Isa 30:19-21; 31:1; 32:5-6 + 30 tiny fragments
4Q*164*	4QpIsa[d]	Commentary on Isa 54:11, 12
4Q*165*	4QpIsa[e]	Commentary on Isa 1:1(?); 40:12; 14:19; 15:4-6; Isa 21:2(?), 11-15; 32:5-7 + fragments
4Q*166*	4QpHos[a]	Commentary on Hos 2:8-9, 10-14
4Q*167*	4QpHos[b]	Commentary on Hos 5:13-15; 6:4, 7, 9-10; 8:13-14 + fragments
4Q*168*	4QpMic	Commentary on Mic 4:8-12
4Q*169*	4QpNah	Commentary on Nah 1:3-6; 2:12-14; 3:1-5, 6-9, 10-12, 14
4Q*170*	4QpZeph	Commentary on Zeph 1:12-13
4Q*171*	4QpPs[a]	Commentary on Ps 37:7, 8-19a, 19b-26, 28c-40; 45:1-2; 60:8-9 (108:8-9)
4Q*172*	4QpUnid	Commentary on unidentified texts
4Q*173*	4QpPs[b]	Commentary on Ps 127:2-3, 5; 129:7-8; 118: 26-27(?)

(B) *Other Texts Using Biblical Passages*

4Q*158*	4QBibParaph	Paraphrase of Gen 32:25-32, 31(?); Exod 4:27-28; 3:12; Gen 24:4-6; Exod 19:17-23; 20:19-22; Deut 5:29; 18:18-20, 22; Exod 20:12, 16, 17; Deut 5:30-31; Exod 20:22-26; 21:1, 3, 4, 6, 8, 10; 21:15, 16, 18, 20, 22, 25, 32, 34, 35-37; 22:1-11, 13; 30:32, 34: (see p. 143 below)
4Q*159*	4QOrd	Ordinances
4Q*160*	4QVisSamuel	Cf. 1 Sam 3:14-17
4Q*174*	4QFlor	Quotations from 2 Sam 7:10-14 (1 Chr 17:9-13); Exod 15:17-18; Amos 9:11; Ps 1:1; Isa 8:11; Ezek 37:23(?); Ps 2:1; Dan 12:10; 11:32 (intervening comments); Deut 33:8-11, 12(?), 19-21 + fragments
4Q*175*	4QTestim	Quotations from Deut 5:28-29; 18:18-19 (= Samaritan Pentateuch Exod 20:21); Num 24:15-17; Deut 33:8-11; Josh 6:26 (+ comments = 4QPssJosh)

4Q*176*	4QTanḥumim	Quotations from Ps 79:2-3; Isa 40:1-5; 41:8-9; 49:7, 13-17; 43:1-2, 4-6; 51:22-23, 23c-e; 52:1-3; 54:4-10; 52:1-2; Zech 13:9 + fragments of comments
4Q*177*	4QCatena^{a}	(Text possibly related to 4QFlor; see J. Strugnell, *RQ* 7 [1969-71] 236-37)
4Q*178*	4Q?	
4Q*179*	4QapLam	Allusions to Lamentations 1 and 4
4Q*180*	4QAgesCreat	(This and the following text are possibly related to 11QMelchizedek)
4Q*181*	4Q?	
4Q*182*	4QCatena^{b}	On Enemies of the Community
4Q*183*	4Q?	Desecration of the Temple (?)
4Q*184*	4QWiles	Instruction of Sapiential Genre
4Q*185*	4Q?	Sapiential Text
4Q*186*	4QCryptic	This is possibly related to the Enoch literature; see J. T. Milik, *HTR* 64 (1971) 366.

D. *Cave 11*

(1) *OT Texts*

11QLev — Ploeg, J. P. M. van der, "Lév. IX,23-X,2 dans un texte de Qumran," *Bibel und Qumran: Beiträge zur Erforschung der Beziehungen zwischen Bibel- und Qumranwissenschaft: Hans Bardtke zum 22. 9. 1966* (ed. S. Wagner; Berlin: Evangelische Haupt-Bibelgesellschaft, 1968) 153-55 (= Lev 9:23-10:2)

11QpaleoLev — Freedman, D. N., "Variant Readings in the Leviticus Scroll from Qumran Cave 11," *CBQ* 36/4 (Patrick W. Skehan Festschrift, 1974) 525-34 (+ photo of Lev 14:53-15:5); gives variants in Lev 15:3; 17:2-4; 18:27-19:3; 20:2-3; 21:6-9; 22:22-25; 24:9-10; 25:29-35; 26:20-24; 27:13-17.

11QEzek — Brownlee, W. H., "The Scroll of Ezekiel from the Eleventh Qumran Cave," *RQ* 4 (1963-64) 11-28 (+ pls. I-II) (= Ezek 4:9, 10; 5:11-17; 7:9-12)

11QPs[a] — Sanders, J. A., *The Psalms Scroll of Qumran Cave 11 (11QPs[a])* (DJD 4; Oxford: Clarendon, 1965); *The Dead Sea Psalms Scroll* (Ithaca: Cornell University, 1967). The postscript of the latter book (pp. 155-65) contains the text of an additional fragment (E), on which see Y. Yadin, "Another Fragment (E) of the Psalms Scroll from Qumran Cave 11 (11QPs[a])," *Textus* 5 (1966) 1-10 (+ pls. I-V) (See the detailed analysis of this scroll below, p. 37)

11QPs[b] — Ploeg, J. van der, "Fragments d'un manuscrit de psaumes de Qumran (11QPs[b])," *RB* 74 (1967) 408-12 (+ pl. XVIII) (= the Plea for Deliverance of 11QPs[a] [19:1-15]; Ps 141:10 [last word only], followed by Ps 133:1-3; Ps 144:1-2; Ps 118:1[?], 5)

11QPsAp[a] — Ploeg, J. van der, "Le psaume xci dans une recension de Qumran," *RB* 72 (1965) 210-17 (+ pls. VIII-IX) (= Ps 91:1-16, which follows on apocryphal psalms); "Un petit rouleau de psaumes apocryphes

(11 QPsAp[a])," *Tradition und Glaube: Das frühe Christentum in seiner Umwelt: Festgabe für Karl Georg Kuhn zum 65. Geburtstag* (eds. G. Jeremias et al.; Göttingen: Vandenhoeck & Ruprecht, 1971) 128-39 (+ pls. II-VII) (= the apocryphal psalms which precede Psalm 91 published in the preceding entry)

(2) *Targum*

11QtgJob Ploeg, J. P. M. van der, and A. S. van der Woude, *Le targum de Job de la grotte XI de Qumrân*, édité et traduit avec la collaboration de B. Jongeling (Koninklijke nederlandse Akademie van Wetenschappen; Leiden: Brill, 1971); cf. M. Sokoloff, *The Targum to Job from Qumran Cave XI* (Bar-Ilan Studies in Near Eastern Languages and Culture; Ramat-Gan: Bar-Ilan University, 1974)

Ploeg, J. van der, "Le targum de Job de la grotte 11 de Qumran (11QtgJob), Première communication," *Mededelingen der koninklijke nederlandse Akademie van Wetenschappen*, Afd. Letterkunde, nieuwe reeks, deel 25, no. 9 (Amsterdam: N. V. Noord-hollandsche Uitgevers Maatschappij, 1962) 543-57 (preliminary report on the preceding entry)

(3) *Apocryphal and Sectarian Texts*

11QMelch Woude, A. S. van der, "Melchisedech als himmlische Erlösergestalt in den neugefundenen eschatologischen Midraschim aus Qumran Höhle XI," *OS* 14 (1965) 354-73. Cf. J. T. Milik, "Milkî-ṣedeq et Milkî-rešaʿ," *JJS* 23 (1972) 96-102, 124-26

11QBer Woude, A. S. van der, "Ein neuer Segensspruch aus Qumran (11QBer)," *Bibel und Qumran: Beiträge zur Erforschung der Beziehungen zwischen Bibel- und Qumranwissenschaft: Hans Bardtke zum 22. 9. 1966* (ed. S. Wagner; Berlin: Evangelische Haupt-Bibelgesellschaft, 1968) 253-58 (+ pl.). Cf.

the review of this volume by J. Strugnell, *RB* 77 (1970) 267-68.

11QJN ar — Jongeling, B., "Publication provisoire d'un fragment provenant de la grotte 11 de Qumrân (11Q Jér Nouv ar)," *JSJ* 1 (1970) 58-64; "Note additionnelle," ibid., 185-86

11QTemple — Yadin, Y., "The Temple Scroll," *New Directions in Biblical Archaeology* (eds. D. N. Freedman and J. C. Greenfield; Garden City: Doubleday, 1969) 139-48 (+ figs. 56-57); derived from *BA* 30 (1967) 135-39; "*Mgylt hmqdš*," *Jerusalem through the Ages: The Twenty-Fifth Archaeological Convention October 1967* (ed. J. Aviram; Jerusalem: Israel Exploration Society, 1968) 72-84 (+ pl. XII)

Yadin, Y., "Pesher Nahum (4Q pNahum) Reconsidered," *IEJ* 21 (1971) 1-12, esp. pp. 5-10 (+ pl. I) (= col. 64:6-13)

Yadin, Y., "L'attitude essénienne envers la polygamie et le divorce," *RB* 79 (1972) 98-99, esp. p. 99 (= col. 57:17-19)

11QJub — Woude, A. S. van der, "Fragmente des Buches Jubiläen aus Qumran Höhle XI (11 Q Jub)," *Tradition und Glaube: Das frühe Christentum in seiner Umwelt: Festgabe für Karl Georg Kuhn zum 65. Geburtstag* (eds. G. Jeremias et al.; Göttingen: Vandenhoeck & Ruprecht, 1971) 140-46 (+ pl. VIII). Cf. J. T. Milik, "A propos de 11QJub," *Bib* 54 (1973) 77-78.

Detailed Analysis of the Contents of 11QPs[a]

frs. A, B, C i	Ps 101:1-8; 102:1-2 (see DJD 4. 19-49)
fr. C ii	Ps 102:18-29; 103:1
fr. D	Ps 109:21-31
fr. E i	Ps 118:25-29; 104:1-6 (see J. A. Sanders, *DSPS*, 160-65)
ii	Ps 104:21-35; 147:1-2
iii	Ps 147:18-20; 105:?, 1-11

col. i	Ps 105:25-45
ii	Ps 146:9-?-10; 148:1-12
iii	Ps 121:1-8; 122:1-9; 123:1-2
iv	Ps 124:7-8; 125:1-5; 126:1-6; 127:1
v	Ps 128:4-6; 129:1-8; 130:1-8; 131:1
vi	Ps 132:8-18; 119:1-6
vii	Ps 119:15-28
viii	Ps 119:37-49
ix	Ps 119:59-73
x	Ps 119:82-96
xi	Ps 119:105-20
xii	Ps 119:128-42
xiii	Ps 119:150-64
xiv	Ps 119:171-76; 135:1-9
xv	Ps 135:17-21; 136:1-16
xvi	Ps 136:26b(?); 118:1(?), 15, 16, 8, 9, ?, 29(?); 145:1-7
xvii	Ps 145:13-21+?
xviii	Syriac Ps II:3-19 (in Hebrew) [= Psalm 154]
xix	Plea for Deliverance (lines 1-18)
xx	Ps 139:8-24; 137:1
xxi	Ps 137:9; 138:1-8; Sir 51:13-20b
xxii	Sir 51:30; Apostrophe to Zion (lines 1b-15); Ps 93:1-3
xxiii	Ps 141:5-10; 133:1-3; 144:1-7
xxiv	Ps 144:15; Syriac Ps III:1-18 (in Hebrew) [= Psalm 155]
xxv	Ps 142:4-8; 143:1-8
xxvi	Ps 149:7-9; 150:1-6; Hymn to the Creator (lines 9-15)
xxvii	2 Sam 23:7 (line 1); David's Compositions (lines 2-11); Ps 140:1-5
xxviii	Ps 134:1-3; LXX 151 A (Syriac Ps I) (lines 3-12), B (lines 13-14) (in Hebrew)

(See J. A. Sanders, "The Qumran Psalms Scroll [11QPs[a]] Reviewed," *On Language, Culture, and Religion: In Honor of Eugene A. Nida* [eds. M. Black and W. A. Smalley; The Hague: Mouton, 1974] 79-99; Woude, A. S. van der, "Die fünf syrischen Psalmen," *Poetische Schriften* [Jüdische Schriften aus hellenistisch-römischer Zeit, 4; Gütersloh: Mohn, 1974] 29-47).

E. *Unidentified Cave*

(1) *Phylacteries*

XQPhyl 1-4 Yadin, Y., "*Tpylyn-šl-r'š mqwmr'n* (X Q Phyl 1-4)," *W. F. Albright Volume* (Eretz-Israel, 9; Jerusalem: Israel Exploration Society, 1969) 60-85

Yadin, Y., *Tefillin from Qumran (X Q Phyl 1-4)* (Jerusalem: Israel Exploration Society and the Shrine of the Book, 1969) (an English and modern Hebrew edition of the phylacteries)

II. MASADA

(1) *OT Texts*

MasGen
MasLev
MasDeut
MasEzek

Yadin, Y., *Masada: Herod's Fortress and the Zealots' Last Stand* (New York: Random House, 1966) 179, 187-89 (preliminary report only)

MasPs

Yadin, Y., "The Excavation of Masada -- 1963/64: Preliminary Report," *IEJ* 15 (1965) 1-120 (+ pls. 1-24), esp. pp. 81-82, 103-4 (= Ps 81:3-85:10; Lev 4:3-8; Gen 46:7-11)

Yadin, Y., Report in *Jerusalem Post*, 20 December 1964 (discovery of MasPs fr. with Ps 150:1-6)

Sanders, J. A., "Pre-Masoretic Psalter Texts," *DSPS*, 143-49, 152

MasSir

Yadin, Y., *"Mgylt bn-Syrʾ šntglth bmṣdh," The E. L. Sukenik Memorial Volume* (Eretz-Israel, 8; Jerusalem: Israel Exploration Society, 1965) 1-45

Yadin, Y., *The Ben Sira Scroll from Masada: With Introduction, Emendations and Commentary* (Jerusalem: Israel Exploration Society and the Shrine of the Book, 1965) (an English and modern Hebrew edition of the text) (= Sir 39:27-44:17c)

Milik, J. T., "Un fragment mal placé dans l'édition du Siracide de Masada," *Bib* 47 (1966) 425-26

Yadin, Y., "The Excavation of Masada," *IEJ* 15 (1965) 108-9; *The Excavation of Masada 1963/64: Preliminary Report* (Jerusalem: Israel Exploration Society, 1965) 103-14

(2) *Apocryphal Texts*

MasJub — Yadin, Y., *Masada: Herod's Fortress*, 179

MasŠirŠabb — Yadin, Y., "The Excavation of Masada," *IEJ* 15 (1965) 81-82, 105-8

(3) *Ostraca, etc.*

MasOstr — Yadin, Y., ibid., 82, 110-14

papMasEp gr
papMas lat

Yadin, Y., *Masada: Herod's Fortress*, 189-91

III. MURABBAʿAT

Mur 1-173 — Benoit, P., J. T. Milik, and R. de Vaux, *Les grottes de Murabbaʿât* (DJD 2; Oxford: Clarendon, 1961) Two parts: 1. Texte; 2. Planches. (Two caves yielded written material: 1Mur: texts 2, 78; 2Mur: texts 3-77, 79-173. But it is customary not to distinguish them by cave in this instance, and the texts are simply designated by Mur and numbered consecutively according to genre.)

Bardtke, H., *Die Handschriftenfunde in der Wüste Juda* (Berlin: Evangelische Haupt-Bibelgesellschaft, 1962)

Koffmahn, E., *Die Doppelurkunden aus der Wüste Juda: Recht und Praxis der jüdischen Papyri des 1. und 2. Jahrhunderts n. Chr. samt Übertragung der Texte und deutsche Übersetzung* (STDJ 5; Leiden: Brill, 1968)

Detailed Listing of Mur 1-173 in DJD 2

A. *Murabbaʿat Cave 1*

Mur 2	Mur Deut	Deut 10:1-3; 11:2-3; 12:25-26; 14:29-15:1 or 2
Mur 78	MurABC[a]	Ostracon with inscribed partial alphabet

B. *Murabbaʿat Cave 2*

(1) *OT Texts*

Mur 1	MurGen, Mur-Exod, MurNum	Gen 32:4-5, 30; 32:33-33:1; 34:5-7; 34:30-35:1, 4-7; Exod 4:28-31; 5:3; 6:5-11; Num 34:10; 36:7-11	
Mur 3	MurIsa	Isa 1:4-14	
Mur 4	MurPhyl	Exod 13:1-10, 11-16; Deut 11:13-21; 6:4-9	
Mur 5	MurMez(?)	Illegible	
Mur 88	MurXII	col. i	Joel 2:20
		ii	Joel 2:26-4:16
		iii	Amos 1:5-2:1

iv-v	(missing)
vi	Amos 6 (only a few letters left)
vii	Amos 7:3-8:7
viii	Amos 8:11-9:15
ix	Obad 1-21
x	Jonah 1:1-3:2
xi	Jonah 3:2 -- Mic 1:5
xii	Mic 1:5-3:4
xiii	Mic 3:4-4:12
xiv	Mic 4:12-6:7
xv	Mic 6:11-7:17
xvi	Mic 7:17 -- Nah 2:12
xvii	Nah 2:13-3:19
xviii	Hab 1:3-2:11
xix	Hab 2:18 -- Zeph 1:1
xx	Zeph 1:11-3:6
xxi	Zeph 3:8 -- Hag 1:11
xxii	Hag 1:12-2:10
xxiii	Hag 2:12 -- Zech 1:4

(2) *Literary Texts (?)*

Mur 6	Mur?	Non-biblical Literary Text
Mur 72	Mur?	Aramaic Narrative Text (written on an ostracon)
Mur 108 gr	Mur?	Fragmentary Philosophical(?) Text (on papyrus)
Mur 109-12 gr		Fragmentary Literary Texts (on papyrus)

(3) *Non-Literary Documents and Letters*

Mur 7		Contract (very fragmentary, in Hebrew)
Mur 8 ar		Account of cereals and vegetables (in Aramaic)
Mur 9		List (with numerical ciphers)
Mur 10	MurPalimp[a]	List of names with accounts; Abecedary
Mur 11		Abecedary
Mur 12-16		Non-classified fragments
Mur 17	papMurPalimp[b]	Palimpsest: Letter (8th c. BC [Milik]); List of persons

Mur 18 ar		IOU (dated in 2nd year of Nero Caesar, AD 55/56) (in Aramaic)
Mur 19 ar		Writ of divorce (in Aramaic, dated AD 111)
Mur 20 ar		Marriage contract (in Aramaic, dated AD 117)
Mur 21 ar		Marriage contract (in Aramaic, date missing [Milik is inclined to date "avant la Première Révolte?"])
Mur 22		Deed of sale of land (in Hebrew, dated AD 131)
Mur 23 ar		Deed of sale(?) (in Aramaic, AD 132[?])
Mur 24		Farming contracts (*diastrōmata*, in Hebrew, AD 133), texts A-F: more or less complete; texts G-L: quite fragmentary
Mur 25 ar		Deed of sale of land (in Aramaic, AD 133)
Mur 26 ar		Deed of sale (in Aramaic)
Mur 27 ar		Deed of sale (in Aramaic)
Mur 28 ar		Deed about some property (in Aramaic)
Mur 29		Deed of sale (in Hebrew, dated AD 133)
Mur 30		Deed of sale of land (in Hebrew, dated AD 134)
Mur 31 ar		Deeds of sale, various fragments (in Aramaic)
Mur 32 ar		Deed about money (in Aramaic)
Mur 33 ar		Deed about money (in Aramaic)
Mur 34-35 ar		Fragments of Aramaic contracts
Mur 36		Fragments of a Hebrew contract
Mur 37-40		Scraps of contracts and signatures
Mur 41		List of persons
Mur 42	MurEpBeth-Mashiko	Letter of the administrators of Beth-Mashiko to Yeshuaʿ ben Galgulaʾ
Mur 43	MurEpBarC[a]	Letter of Shimʿon ben Kosibah to Yeshuaʿ ben Galgulaʾ
Mur 44	MurEpBarC[b]	Letter of Shimʿon to Yeshuaʿ ben Galgulaʾ
Mur 45		Letter (fragmentary)
Mur 46	MurEpJonathan	Letter of Jonathan ben X to Joseph [ben...], sent from ʿEn-Gedi
Mur 47		Fragmentary letter (in Hebrew)

Mur 48	Fragmentary letter (in Hebrew)
Mur 49-52	Fragments of letters
Mur 53-70	Non-classified fragments
Mur 71 nab	Fragment of a text written in Nabatean script
Mur 73	Abecedary and list of personal names on an ostracon
Mur 74	List of persons on an ostracon
Mur 75-77	Lists of persons on ostraca
Mur 79-80	Abecedaries on ostraca
Mur 81-86	Non-classified fragments of ostraca
Mur 87	Personal name on an ostracon
Mur 89 gr	Account of money (in Greek, on skin)
Mur 90 gr	Account of cereals and vegetables (in Greek, on skin)
Mur 91 gr	Account of cereals and vegetables (in Greek, on skin)
Mur 92 gr	Account of cereals (in Greek, on skin)
Mur 93 gr	An account of (?) (in Greek, on skin)
Mur 94 gr	Recapitulation of accounts (in Greek, on skin)
Mur 95 gr	List of names (in Greek, on skin)
Mur 96 gr	Account of cereals and vegetables (in Greek, on skin)
Mur 97 gr	Account of cereals (in Greek, on skin)
Mur 98-102 gr	Fragments of accounts (?)
Mur 103-7 gr	"Coins de feuilles et onglets" (in Greek, on skin)
Mur 113 gr	Proceedings of a lawsuit
Mur 114 gr	IOU (in Greek, on papyrus, dated AD 171[?])
Mur 115 gr	Contract of remarriage (in Greek, *Doppelurkunde* on papyrus, dated AD 124)
Mur 116 gr	Contract of marriage (in Greek, on papyrus)
Mur 117 gr	Extracts of official ordinances (in Greek, on papyrus, end of 2d c. AD)
Mur 118 gr	An account (fragmentary, on papyrus, in Greek)
Mur 119 gr	A list (fragmentary, on papyrus, in Greek)

Mur 120 gr	A list (fragmentary, on papyrus, in Greek)
Mur 121 gr	A list (fragmentary, on papyrus, in Greek)
Mur 122 gr	A list or a schoolboy's exercise (in Greek, on papyrus)
Mur 123-25 gr	Fragments of lists
Mur 126-32 gr	Fragments in literary or notarial script
Mur 133-54	Fragments in cursive script
Mur 155 gr	Fragments of a document
Mur 156 gr	Christian liturgical fragment (11th c. AD [?])
Mur 157 gr	Fragmentary magical text (10th c. AD)
Mur 158-59 lat	Fragmentary texts of official nature (in Latin, on papyrus)
Mur 160-63 lat	Fragments (in Latin, on papyrus)
Mur 164 gr	Document in Greek shorthand (as yet undeciphered)
Mur 165-68	Ostraca texts (very fragmentary) in Greek or Latin
Mur 169-73	Arabic texts (from the 9th-10th c. AD)

IV. NAḤAL ḤEVER (WADI ḪABRA)

Cf. *The Expedition to the Judean Desert, 1960-1961* (= *IEJ* 11-12 [1961-62])

(1) *OT Texts*

?ḤevGen	Burchard, C., "Gen 35:6-10 und 36:5-12 MT aus der Wüste Juda (Naḥal Ḥever, Cave of the Letters?)," *ZAW* 78 (1966) 71-75 (The photograph is published in *ADAJ* 2 [1953] pl. XII)
5/6ḤevPs	Yadin, Y., "Expedition D," *IEJ* 11 (1961) 36-52, esp. p. 40 (= Ps 15:1-5; 16:1 [and even 7:14-31:22; cf. J. A. Sanders, *JBL* 86 (1967) 439])
5/6ḤevNum	Yadin, Y., "Expedition D -- The Cave of the Letters," *IEJ* 12 (1962) 227-57, esp. p. 229 (+ pl. 48; = Num 20:7-8)
8ḤevXII gr	Barthélemy, D., *Les devanciers d'Aquila: Première publication intégrale du texte des fragments du Dodécaprophéton trouvés dans le Désert de Juda, précédée d'une étude sur les traductions et recensions grecques de la Bible réalisées au premier siècle de notre ère sous l'influence du rabbinat palestinien* (VTSup 10; Leiden: Brill, 1963) 163-78

Detailed Listing of Contents of 8ḤevXII gr

col.	i	Jon 1:14, 16; 2:1, 4-7
	ii	Jon 3:7-10; 4:1-2, 5
	iii	Mic 1:1-7
	iv	Mic 1:7-8
	v	Mic 2:7-8; 3:5-6
	vi	Mic 4:3-5
	vii	Mic 4:6-10; 5:1-4
	viii	Mic 5:4-6
	ix	Nah 2:5-14
	x	Nah 3:6-17
	xi	Hab 1:5-11
	xii	Hab 1:14-17; 2:1-8
	xiii	Hab 2:13-20

xiv	Hab 3:9-15
xv	Zeph 1:1-5
xvi	Zeph 1:13-17
xvii	Zeph 2:9-10
xviii	Zeph 3:6-7
xix	Zech 1:1, 3-4
xx	Zech 1:13-14
xxi	Zech 2:2, 7
xxii	Zech 2:16-17; 3:1, 4-7
xxiii	Zech 8:19-23
xxiv	Zech 8:24-9:4

8ḤevXII gr Lifshitz, B., "The Greek Documents from the Cave of Horror," *IEJ* 12 (1962) 201-7 (+ pl. 32B); *Yediʿot* 26 (1962) 183-90 (9 more fragments belonging to the text that Barthélemy published, discovered in March 1961, establishing the provenience of the text). Barthélemy (*Les devanciers d'Aquila*, 168, n. 9) differs with Lifshitz' identification of the frs. and proposes the following identification:

fr. 1	Nah 3:13 (Lifshitz: Hos 2:8)
fr. 2	Amos 1:5 (?) (Lifshitz: Amos 1:5)
fr. 3	Nah 1:14 (Lifshitz: Joel 1:14)
fr. 4	Jonah 3:2-5 (also Lifshitz)
fr. 5	Nah 1:13-14 (Lifshitz: Nah 1:9)
fr. 6	? (certainly not Nah 2:8-9 [so Lifshitz]; see above)
fr. 7	Zech 3:1-2 (also Lifshitz)
fr. 8	Nah 3:3 (Lifshitz: 3:1-2)
fr. 9	Zech 2:11-12 (Lifshitz: Zech 4:8-9)

(2) *Letters and Contracts*

pap5/6ḤevA nab Starcky, J., "Un contrat nabatéen sur papyrus," *RB* 61 (1954) 161-81; cf. Y. Yadin, "Expedition D -- The Cave of the Letters," *IEJ* 12 (1962) 227-57, esp. p. 229 (on the provenience of the contract) pap?Ḥev B ar — Milik, J. T., "Un contrat juif de l'an 134 après J.-C.," *RB* 61 (1954) 182-90; "Deux documents inédits du Désert de Juda," *Bib* 38 (1957) 245-68, esp. pp. 264-68 (+ pl. IV)

pap?Ḥev C ar — Milik, J. T., "Deux documents," *Bib* 38 (1957) 255-64 (+ pls. II-III)

5/6Ḥev Ep 1-15 — Yadin, Y., "Expedition D," *IEJ* 11 (1961) 36-52 (+ pl. 22); *BIES* (= *Yediʿot*) 25 (1961) 49-64; "Expedition D -- The Cave of the Letters," *IEJ* 12 (1962) 227-57. Cf. E. Y. Kutscher, "The Languages of the Hebrew and Aramaic Letters of Bar Kokhba and His Contemporaries," *Lešonénu* 25 (1960-61) 117-33; 26 (1961-62) 7-23 [texts of various letters with brief modern Hebrew commentary]

5/6Ḥev BA — Yadin, Y., "Expedition D -- The Cave of Letters," *IEJ* 12 (1962) 227-57, esp. pp. 235-57 (mostly a preliminary report, but with some texts of the Babatha archive)

5/6Ḥev BA — Polotsky, H. J., "*Šlwš tʿwdwt m'rkywnh šl Bbth bt Šmʿwn*," *The E. L. Sukenik Memorial Volume* (Eretz-Israel, 8; Jerusalem: Israel Exploration Society, 1967) 46-51 (3 documents of the Babatha archive)

Yadin, Y., "The Nabataean Kingdom, Provincia Arabia, Petra and En-Geddi in the Documents from Naḥal Ḥever," *JEOL* 17 (1963) 227-41

Polotsky, H. J., "The Greek Papyri from the Cave of the Letters," *IEJ* 12 (1962) 258-62; *Yediʿot* 26 (1962) 237-41

Yadin, Y., *Bar-Kokhba: The Rediscovery of the Legendary Hero of the Second Jewish Revolt against Rome* (London: Weidenfeld and Nicolson, 1971) 124-253

5/6Ḥev Ep gr — Lifshitz, B., "Papyrus grecs du désert de Juda," *Aegyptus* 42 (1962) 240-56 (+ 2 pls.); cf. Y. Yadin, *Bar-Kokhba*, 130-31 (2 Greek letters of Bar Cochba or his lieutenant)

8ḤevEp gr Aharoni, Y., "Expedition B -- The Cave of Horror," *IEJ* 12 (1962) 186-99, esp. p. 197; cf. B. Lifshitz, "The Greek Documents," *IEJ* 12 (1962) 206-7 (+ pl. 32A)

V. NAḤAL ṢE'ELIM (WADI SEIYAL)

34ṢePhyl	Aharoni, Y., "Expedition B," *IEJ* 11 (1961) 11-24, esp. pp. 22-23 (+ pl. 11); *Yediʿot* 25 (1961) 19-33; cf. *ILN*, 20 February 1960, p. 230 (Photograph); London *Times*, 16 February, 1960 (= 2 phylactery fragments, Exod 13:2-10, 11-16)
34ṢeEp	Aharoni, Y., "Expedition B," *IEJ* 11 (1961) 11-24, esp. p. 24
pap34Ṣe gr 1-8	Lifshitz, B., "The Greek Documents from Naḥal Ṣeelim and Naḥal Mishmar," *IEJ* 11 (1961) 53-62, esp. pp. 53-58 (+ pl. 23), 205; *BIES* (= *Yediʿot*) 25 (1961) 65-73 (lists of Greek names)

VI. NAḤAL MISHMAR (WADI MAHRAS)

paplMiš gr — Bar Adon, P., "Expedition C," *IEJ* 11 (1961) 25-35; *BIES* 25 (1961) 34-38

Lifshitz, B., "The Greek Documents from Naḥal Ṣeelim and Naḥal Mishmar," *IEJ* 11 (1961) 53-62, esp. pp. 59-60 (papyrus lists of names)

VII. Ḫ IRBET MIRD

papMird A	Milik, J. T., "Une inscription et une lettre en araméen christo-palestinien," *RB* 60 (1953) 526-39; cf. *Bib* 42 (1961) 21-27
Mird Acts cpa	Perrot, C., "Un fragment christo-palestinien découvert à Khirbet Mird (Actes des Apôtres, X, 28-29; 32-41)," *RB* 70 (1963) 506-55 (+ pls. XVIII, XIX)
papMird 1-100 arab	Grohmann, A., *Arabic Papyri from Ḫirbet el-Mird* (Bibliothèque du Muséon, 52; Louvain: Publications universitaires, 1963)

VIII. CAIRO GENIZAH

Though not discovered in the vicinity of the Dead Sea, these texts are medieval copies of some of the documents that have been discovered in the Qumran caves or at Masada and are thus related to them. These texts were actually found at the end of the 19th century in a genizah of the Ezra Synagogue in Old Cairo.

CSir — Schechter, S. and C. Taylor, *The Wisdom of Ben Sira: Portions of the Book Ecclesiasticus from Hebrew Manuscripts in the Cairo Genizah Collection Presented to the University of Cambridge by the Editors* (Cambridge: Cambridge University, 1899)

CD — Schechter, S., *Documents of Jewish Sectaries: Vol. 1: Fragments of a Zadokite Work* (Cambridge: Cambridge University, 1910) [reprinted with a prolegomenon by J. A. Fitzmyer; New York: Ktav, 1970].

Zeitlin, S., *The Zadokite Fragments: Facsimile of the Manuscripts in the Cairo Genizah Collection in the Possession of the University Library, Cambridge, England* (Jewish Quarterly Review, Monograph Series, 1; Philadelphia: Dropsie College, 1952).

CTLevi ar — Grelot, P., "Le testament araméen de Lévi, est-il traduit de l'hébreu? A propos du fragment de Cambridge, col. c 10 à d 1," *REJ* 114 (1955) 91-99. (Cf. *RB* 62 [1955] 398-406)

3

BIBLIOGRAPHIES OF THE DEAD SEA SCROLLS

BIBLIOGRAPHIES OF THE DEAD SEA SCROLLS

LaSor, W. S., *Bibliography of the Dead Sea Scrolls 1948-1957* (Fuller Library Bulletin, 31; Pasadena: Fuller Theological Seminary Library, 1958)
[Topical arrangement]

Burchard, C., *Bibliographie zu den Handschriften vom Toten Meer* (BZAW 76; Berlin: Töpelmann, 1957)
[Alphabetical arrangement]

Bibliographie zu den Handschriften vom Toten Meer, II: Nr. 1557-4459 (BZAW 89; Berlin: Töpelmann, 1965)
[Continuation of the preceding; up to 1962]

Yizhar, M., *Bibliography of Hebrew Publications on the Dead Sea Scrolls 1948-1964* (HTS 23; Cambridge: Harvard University, 1967)
[Topical arrangement; see my review, *JBL* 87 (1968) 116]

Jongeling, B., *A Classified Bibliography of the Finds in the Desert of Judah -- 1958-1969* (STDJ 7; Leiden: Brill, 1971).
[Sequel to LaSor's *Bibliography*; topical arrangement]

(Various Authors), "Bibliographie," *RQ* 1 (1958-59) 149-60 (J. Carmignac), 309-20 (J. C.), 461-79 (C. Burchard), 547-626 (C. B.); 2 (1959-60) 117-51 (C. B.), 299-312 (J. C.), 459-72 (W. S. LaSor), 587-601 (W. S. L.); 3 (1961-62) 149-60 (W. S. L.), 313-20 (W. S. L.), 467-80 (W. S. L.), 593-602 (W. S. L.); 4 (1963-64) 139-59 (W. S. L.), 311-20 (W. S. L.), 467-80 (W. S. L.), 597-606 (J. C.); 5 (1964-66) 149-60 (W. S. L.), 293-320 (W. S. L.), 463-79 (J. C.), 597-607 (J. C.); 6 (1967-69) 301-20 (J. C.), 457-79 (J. C.); 7 (1969-71) 131-59 (J. C.), 305-19 (J. C.), 463-80 (J. C.); 8 (1972-) 131-59 (J. C.), 299-319 (J. C.), 459-79 (J. C.)
[Neither alphabetical nor topical arrangement; listed by periodicals from which the entries are culled (?!)]

Habermann, A. M., "*Byblywgrpyh lḥqr mgylwt mdbr yhwdh wš'r hmmṣ'ym šnmṣ'w šm*" [title varies in different installments], *Beth*

Mikra (Jerusalem) 1 (1956) 116-21; 2 (1957) 92-97; 3 (1958) 103-11; 4 (1959) 91-95; 5 (1960) 89-93; 6 (1961) 87-91; 13 (1962) 126-33; 16 (1963) 147-51; Nos. 18-19 (1964) 215-19; Nos. 23-24 (1965) 125-33; No. 27 (1966) 162-67; No. 32 (1967) 134-36; No. 35 (1968) 134-40; No. 41 (1969-70) 208-16; (nothing in Nos. 42-51 [1972])
[Alphabetical arrangement]

Nober, P., "Elenchus bibliographicus," *Biblica*, each year up to 1967, section IV/c, "Qumranica et praemishnica"; since 1968 the bibliography has been published each year separately as *Elenchus bibliographicus biblicus* (Rome: Biblical Institute), see section IV/3.
[Alphabetical arrangement]

Fitzmyer, J. A., "A Bibliographical Aid to the Study of the Qumran Cave IV Texts 158-186," *CBQ* 31 (1969) 59-71 (serves as a supplement to DJD 5)
[Arranged according to texts]

4

SURVEY ARTICLES AND PRELIMINARY REPORTS ON UNPUBLISHED MATERIALS

SURVEY ARTICLES AND PRELIMINARY REPORTS ON UNPUBLISHED MATERIALS

Baillet, M. et al., "Le travail d'édition des fragments manuscrits de Qumrân," *RB* 63 (1956) 49-67 (Report on 2-6Q)

Benoit, P. et al., "Editing the Manuscript Fragments from Qumran," *BA* 19 (1956) 75-96 (An English version of the preceding)

Milik, J. T., "Le travail d'édition des manuscrits du Désert de Juda," *Volume du Congrès, Strasbourg 1956* (VTSup 4; Leiden: Brill, 1957) 17-26 (Report on Murabbaʿat, Ḥever, Minor Caves, 4Q texts)

Milik, J. T., *Ten Years of Discovery in the Wilderness of Judaea* (SBT 26; Naperville, IL: Allenson, 1959) 20-43 ("The Qumran Library")

Hunzinger, C.-H., "Qumran," *Evangelisches Kirchenlexikon* (Göttingen: Vandenhoeck & Ruprecht), 3 (1959) 420-30

Cross, F. M., *The Ancient Library of Qumran and Modern Biblical Studies* (rev. ed.; Anchor Books A 272; Garden City, NY: Doubleday, 1961) 30-47 ("A Catalogue of the Library of Qumran")

Cross, F. M., *Die antike Bibliothek von Qumran und die moderne biblische Wissenschaft: Ein zusammenfassender Überblick über die Handschriften vom Toten Meer und ihre einstigen Besitzer* (Neukirchener Studienbücher, 5; Neukirchen/Vluyn: Neukirchener Verlag, 1967) (An updated form of *ALQ*)

Aviram, J. et al., *The Judean Desert Caves Archaeological Survey, 1961* (= *Yediʿot* 26/3-4; Jerusalem: Hebrew University and Department of Antiquities, 1963) (in modern Hebrew)

Avigad, N. et al., *The Expedition to the Judean Desert, 1961* (= *IEJ* 12/3-4; Jerusalem: Israel Exploration Society, 1962)

Skehan, P. W., "The Biblical Scrolls from Qumran and the Text of the Old Testament," *BA* 28 (1965) 87-100

Brown, R. E., "Apocrypha; Dead Sea Scrolls; Other Jewish Literature," *The Jerome Biblical Commentary* (eds. R. E. Brown, J. A. Fitzmyer, and R. E. Murphy; Englewood Cliffs, NJ: Prentice-Hall, 1968), art. 68 (2. 535-60, esp. pp. 546-57)

Yadin, Y., *Bar-Kokhba: The Rediscovery of the Legendary Hero of the Second Jewish Revolt against Rome* (London: Weidenfeld and Nicolson, 1971) 124-253

Sanders, J. A., "The Dead Sea Scrolls -- A Quarter Century of Study," *BA* 36 (1973) 110-48

5

LISTS OF THE DEAD SEA SCROLLS AND FRAGMENTS

LISTS OF THE DEAD SEA SCROLLS AND FRAGMENTS

The lists mentioned below are similar to that of section 2 above, but they are often less complete; some, however, include notice of texts known to exist but not yet published. Each list has its advantages and disadvantages, and the mode of listing in one reveals aspects of the study not found in others.

Burchard, C., *Bibliographie II* (see section 3 above), 313-59: "Register: Ausgaben und Übersetzungen der neugefundenen Texte, Antike Essenerberichte"

Stegemann, H., "Anhang," *ZDPV* 83 (1967) 95-100 (a supplement to Burchard's list)

Sanders, J. A., "Pre-Masoretic Psalter Texts," *CBQ* 27 (1965) 114-23

Sanders, J. A., *DSPS*, 143-49: "Appendix II: Pre-Masoretic Psalter Texts" (cf. *JBL* 86 [1967] 439 for corrections)

Sanders, J. A., "Palestinian Manuscripts 1947-67," *JBL* 86 (1967) 431-40

Sanders, J. A., "Palestinian Manuscripts 1947-1972," *JJS* 24 (1973) 74-83

Brown, R. E., "Apocrypha" (see section 4 above) #69 (p. 548)

Müller, K., "Die Handschriften und Editionen der ausserbiblischen Qumranliteratur," *Einführung in die Methoden der biblischen Exegese* (ed. J. Schreiner; Würzburg: Echter Verlag, 1971) 303-10

6

CONCORDANCES AND DICTIONARIES FOR THE STUDY OF THE DEAD SEA SCROLLS

CONCORDANCES AND DICTIONARIES FOR THE STUDY OF THE DEAD SEA SCROLLS

These books are intended for use in the study of the original texts (in Aramaic, Hebrew, or Greek). They presuppose the use of ordinary concordances and dictionaries in the study of these biblical languages.

Kuhn, K. G. et al., *Konkordanz zu den Qumrantexten* (Göttingen: Vandenhoeck & Ruprecht, 1960). (All extrabiblical texts of 1Q; 4QIsa^{a-d}, 4QHos^{a,b}, 4QpNah, 4QpPs37, 4QPBless, 4QFlor, 4QTestim, 4QM^{a}, 6QD, CD)

Kuhn, K. G. et al., "Nachträge zur 'Konkordanz zu den Qumrantexten,'" *RQ* 4 (1963-64) 163-234 (4QpNah, 4QpPs37, 4QFlor, 4QŠirŠabb, 4QDibHam, 4QOrd)

Habermann, A. M., *Megilloth Midbar Yehuda: The Scrolls from the Judean Desert, Edited with Vocalization, Introduction, Notes and Concordance* (Tel Aviv: Machbaroth Lesifruth, 1959) [1]-[175]

Lignée, H., "Concordance de '1 Q Genesis Apocryphon,'" *RQ* 1 (1958-59) 163-86.

Carmignac, J., "Concordance de la 'Règle de la Guerre,'" *RQ* 1 (1958-59) 7-49.

Kuhn, K. G. et al., *Rückläufiges hebräisches Wörterbuch* (Göttingen: Vandenhoeck & Ruprecht, 1958). (A reverse-index of words in biblical and Qumran Hebrew writings; it lists the words spelled backwards as an aid to the restoration of lacunae in texts)

7

SECONDARY COLLECTIONS OF QUMRAN TEXTS

SECONDARY COLLECTIONS OF QUMRAN TEXTS

Listed here are manuals which have brought together various texts of Qumran in convenient form. Sometimes they are accompanied by translations into a modern language; sometimes they are vocalized.

Habermann, A. M., *'Edah we-'eduth: Three Scrolls from the Judaean Desert: The Legacy of a Community, Edited with Vocalization, Introduction, Notes and Indices* (Jerusalem: Mahbaroth le-Sifruth, 1952). (Contains 1QpHab, 1QS, CD, and a text from the Cairo Genizah, published by I. Levi, *REJ* 65 [1913] 24-31)

Bardtke, H., *Hebräische Konsonantentexte aus biblischem und ausserbiblischem Schrifttum für Übungszwecke ausgewählt* (Leipzig: Harrassowitz; 1954) (Parts of 1QIsa[a], 1QS, 1QpHab, 1QH, CD, Mur 42, 43)

Boccaccio, P. and G. Berardi (eds. of a series, "Materiale didattico"):

Srk h'dh: Regula congregationis (Fani, Italy: Seminarium Picenum; Rome: Biblical Institute, 1956)

Mlḥmt bny 'wr bbny ḥwšk: Bellum filiorum lucis contra filios tenebrarum: Fasc. A: Transcriptio et versio latina (Fani: Seminarium Picenum, 1956)

Pšr ḥbqwq: Interpretatio Habacuc (1QpHab): Transcriptio et versio latina (Appendix: Interpretatio Nahum [*2, 12b-14*]) (Fani: Seminarium Picenum, 1958). (Second printing contains also *Interpretatio Ps 37.8-11, 19b-26* [Fani: Seminarium Picenum; Rome: Biblical Institute, 1958])

Srk hyḥd: Regula unionis seu manuale disciplinae (1QS): Transcriptio et versio latina (3d ed.; Fani: Seminarium Picenum; Rome: Biblical Institute, 1958)

Habermann, A. M., *Megilloth Midbar Yehudah* (see section 6 above) (The texts incorporated here are pointed)

Lohse, E., *Die Texte aus Qumran: Hebräisch und deutsch, mit masoretischer Punktation, Übersetzung, Einführung und Anmerkungen* (Munich: Kösel; Darmstadt: Wissenschaftliche Buchgesellschaft, 1964; second edition, 1971)

Licht, J., *Mgylt hsrkym: Srk hyḥd, srk lkwl ʿdt yśrʾl lʾḥryt hymym, srk hbrkwt* (Jerusalem: Student Association of Hebrew University, 1961-62) (Annotated unpointed Hebrew text of 1QS, 1QSa, 1QSb)

Weiss, R., *Hmqrʾ bqwmrʾn* (Jerusalem: Hebrew University, 1966) (A collection of samples of the biblical texts used at Qumran: e.g., 1QLev [= 1Q*3*] frs. 1-7; 4QExod[a]; 4QExod[m]; 4QSam[a]; samples of biblical quotations in non-biblical writings of Qumran; cols. 1, 29-33 of 1QIsa[a]; 1QIsa[b]; 11QPs[a] cols. 16-19, 21-22, 24, 27-28; 1QpHab cols. 1-13; 4QpNah cols. 1-4; 4QpPs[a] [= 4QpPs37] cols. 1-4; CD 3:13-4:21; 5:12-6:13; 7:9-21; 1QS cols. 1-11; 1QH col. 5)

Anon., *Tʿwdwt ltwldwt kt mdbr-yhwdh: Documents Bearing on the History of the Judaean Desert Sect* (Jerusalem: Hebrew University, 1966) (contains unpointed Hebrew text of CD, 1QS, 1QSa) [N.B. The title page reads: "For the use of the students of The Hebrew University but not for genaral (sic) sale."]

8

TRANSLATIONS OF THE DEAD SEA SCROLLS IN COLLECTIONS

TRANSLATIONS OF THE DEAD SEA SCROLLS IN COLLECTIONS

Listed here are the books in which one finds formal attempts to translate into a modern language various Qumran texts known at the time, as well as the more wide-ranging discussions of the Scrolls which often incorporate sizeable portions of the texts in translation. Any serious study of the texts must take such translations into consideration as well as those in the formal commentaries on single texts, since they often bear witness to pioneer attempts to cope with the problems of translating the texts of the Dead Sea Scrolls. Translations of single texts, which form part of commentaries on such texts, are not listed here.

Allegro, J. M., *The Dead Sea Scrolls* (Pelican A376; Baltimore: Penguin, 1956)
(partial tr. of 4QSam^{a}, 4QDeut^{a}, 1QS, 1QH, Mur 42-43)

Allegro, J. M., *The Dead Sea Scrolls: A Reappraisal* (Pelican A376; Baltimore: Penguin, 1964)
(partial tr. of 1QS, 1QSa, 1QH, Mur 42-43)

Amusin, I. D., *Nakhodki u Mertvogo moria* (Moscow: Akademia Nauk, 1964)

Amusin, I. D., *Teksty Kumrana* (Moscow: Akademia Nauk, 1971)
(tr. of 1QpHab, 4QpNah, 4QpHos^{b,a}, 1QpMic, 4QpPs37, 4QFlor, 4QBless, 11QMelch, 4QTestim, 1QMyst, 4QPrNab)

Bardtke, H., *Die Handschriftenfunde am Toten Meer: Die Sekte von Qumran* (2d ed.; Berlin: Evangelische Haupt-Bibelgesellschaft, 1961)
(tr. of 1QIsa^{a}, 1QS, 1QM, 1QH, CD, 1QapGen, 1QSa,b, 1Q*34*, 1QDM, 1QMyst, 1QpHab, 1QpMic, 1QpZeph, 1QpPs, 4QPrNab, 4QpNah, 4QFlor, 4QTestim)

Bardtke, H., *Die Handschriftenfunde am Toten Meer: Mit einer kurzen Einführung in die Text- und Kanonsgeschichte des Alten Testaments* (2d ed.; Berlin: Evangelische Haupt-Bibelgesellschaft, 1953)
(tr. of 1QS, 1QH, 1QM, 1QpHab)

Baron, S. W. and J. Blau, *Judaism: Post-Biblical and Talmudic Period* (Library of Religion, 3; New York: Liberal Arts Press, 1954)
(tr. in part of CD, 1QS, 1QH)

Bič, M., *Poklad v Judské poušti: Kumránské nálezy* (Prague: Ustrední církevní nakladaleství, 1960)

Bonsirven, J., *La Bible apocryphe: En marge de l'Ancien Testament* (Paris: Beauchesne, 1953)
(partial tr. of CD, 1QpHab, 1QS, 1QM, 1QH)

Burrows, M., *The Dead Sea Scrolls* (New York: Viking, 1955)
(tr. of CD, 1QpHab, 1QS, 1QM [selections], 1QH [selections])

Burrows, M., *More Light on the Dead Sea Scrolls: New Scrolls and New Interpretations with Translations of Important Recent Discoveries* (New York: Viking, 1958)
(tr. of 1QapGen, 1QSa, 1QSb, 1QMyst, 1QLitPr, 4QPrNab, 4QTestim, 4QFlor, 4QpPs37, 4QPBless, 4QpIsa^{a}, 1QpMic, 4QpNah)

Carmignac, J., P. Guilbert, and E. Cothenet, *Les textes de Qumran traduits et annotés* (2 vols.; Paris: Letouzey et Ané, 1961, 1963)
(tr. of 1QS, 1QM, 1QH, 1QSa, 1QSb, 3QpIsa, 4QpIsa^{b}, 4QpIsa^{a}, 4QpIsa^{c}, 4QpIsa^{d}, 4QpHos^{b}, 4QpHos^{a}, 1QpMic, 4QpNah, 1QpHab, 1QpZeph, 4QpPs37, CD, 1QapGen, 1QDirMo, 1QMyst, 1QLitPr, 4QTestim, 4QFlor, 4QPBless, 4QPrNab, 4QDibHam, 4QŠirŠabb)

Dupont-Sommer, A., *Les écrits esséniens découverts près de la Mer Morte* (Bibliothèque historique; Paris: Payot, 1959; 3d. ed., 1964)
(tr. of 1QS, 1QSa, 1QSb, CD, 1QM, 1QH, 1QpHab, 4QpNah, 4QpPs37, 4QpIsa^{a}, 4QpHos^{b}, 1QpMic, 1QpZeph, 1QapGen, 1QDirMo, 4QFlor, 4QPBless, 4QTestim, 4QpsDan, 4QPrNab, 1QMyst, 1QJN, 1QLitPr)

Dupont-Sommer, A., *The Essene Writings from Qumran* (tr. G. Vermes; Oxford: Blackwell, 1961; reprinted, Cleveland: World, 1962; Magnolia, MA: Peter Smith, 1971)
(tr. of the preceding)

Dupont-Sommer, A., *Aperçus préliminaires sur les manuscrits de la Mer Morte* (L'Orient ancien illustré, 4; Paris: Maisonneuve, 1950)
(tr. [broken up] of 1QpHab, 1QS, CD, 1QH, 1QM)

Dupont-Sommer, A., *The Dead Sea Scrolls: A Preliminary Survey* (tr. E. M. Rowley; Oxford: Blackwell, [1952])
(tr. of the preceding)

Edelkoort, A. H., *De Handschriften van de Dode Zee* (Baarn: Bosch en Keuning, 1952; 2d ed., 1954)
(tr. of 1QpHab, 1QS, 1QH, 1QM, $1QJub^a$)

Gaster, T. H., *The Dead Sea Scriptures in English Translation with Introduction and Notes* (Anchor A378; Garden City, NY: Doubleday, 1956; rev. ed., 1964)
(tr. of 1QS, CD, 1QSb, 1QH, 1Q22, $4QpIsa^a$, $4QpHos^b$, 1QpMic, 4QpNah, 1QpHab, 4QpPs37, 1QapGen, 1QDirMo, 1QM, 1QSa, 1QLitPr, 1QMyst, 4QTestim, 4QFlor, 4QŠirŠabb, 4QDibHam)

Haapa, E. (ed.), *Qumran: Kuolleen meren löydöt 1950-luvun tutkimuksessa* (Porvoo-Helsinki: W. Söderström, 1960)

De Handschriften van de Dode Zee in Nederlands Vertaling (Amsterdam: Proost en Brandt). A series:

A. S. van der Woude, *De Dankpsalmen* (1957) (tr. of 1QH)

A. S. van der Woude, *Bijbelcommentaren en Bijbelse Verhalen* (1958)
(tr. of 1QpHab, 1QpMic, 4QpNah, 4QpPs37, $4QpIsa^a$, 4QPBless, 4QFlor, 4QTestim, 1QapGen, 1QDirMo)

H. A. Brongers, *De Gedragsregels der Qoemraan-Gemeente* (1958)
(tr. of CD, 1QS, 1QSa)

H. A. Brongers, *De Rol van de Strijd* (1960)
(tr. of 1QM)

Hempel, J., "Chronik," *ZAW* 62 (1949-50) 246-72
(partial tr. of 1QM, 1QH)

Lambert, G., "Traduction de quelques 'psaumes' de Qumrân et du 'pêsher' d'Habacuc," *NRT* 74 (1952) 284-97.

Lamadrid, A. G., *Los descubrimientos de Qumran* (Madrid: Instituto español de estudios eclesiásticos, 1956)
(tr. of 1QS, 1QSa, CD, 1QH 3-4, 1QM [in part])

Lamadrid, A. G., *Los descubrimientos del Mar Muerto: Balance de veinticinco años de hallazgos y estudio* (Biblioteca de autores cristianos, 317; Madrid: Editorial católica, 1971)
(partial tr. of major texts)

Lohse, E., *Die Texte aus Qumran hebräisch und deutsch* (see section 7 above)
(tr. of 1QS, 1QSa, 1QSb, CD, 1QH, 1QM, 1QpHab, 4QPBless, 4QTestim, 4QFlor, 4QpNah, 4QpPs37)

Maier, J., *Die Texte vom Toten Meer: I. Übersetzung; II. Anmerkungen* (2 vols.; Munich: E. Reinhardt, 1960)
(tr. of 1QS, CD, 1QH, 1QM, 1QpHab, 1QapGen, 1QpMic, 1QDir-Mo, 1QMyst, 1QSa, 1QSb, 4QpNah, 4QpPs37, 4QPBless, 4QTes-tim, 4QFlor, 4QIsa^{a,b,c,d}, 4QpHos^{a,b})

Medico, H. E. del, *Deux manuscrits hébreux de la Mer Morte: Essai de traduction du 'Manuel de Discipline' et du 'Commentaire d'Habbakuk' avec notes et commentaires* (Paris: Geuthner, 1951)
(tr. of 1QpHab, 1QS)

Medico, H. E. del, *L'énigme des manuscrits de la Mer Morte: Etude sur la provenance et le contenu des manuscrits découverts dans la grotte I de Qumrân suivi de la traduction commentée des principaux textes* (Paris: Plon, 1957)

Medico, H. E. del, *The Riddle of the Scrolls* (tr. H. Garner; London: Burke, 1958)
(tr. of 1QS, 1QSa, 1QSb, 1QpHab, 1QM, 1QH, 1QapGen, CD)

Michelini Tocci, F., *I manoscritti del Mar Morto: Introduzione, traduzione e commento* (Bari: Laterza, 1967)
(tr. of 1QS, 1QSa, 1QSb, CD, 1QM, 1QH, 4QŠirŠabb, 4QDibHam, 1QLitPr, 11QPs^{a}, 4QpPs37, 4QpHos, 1QpMic, 4QpNah, 1QpHab, 3QpIsa, 4QpIsa^{a}, 1QapGen, 4QPrNab, 1QDirMo, 4QTestim, 4QFlor, 4QOrd, 4QPBless, 11QMelch, 1QMyst, 5QJN, 4QMess aram^{a}, 4QCryptic, 4QWiles, 3Q*15*)

Milik, J. T., "Elenchus textuum ex caverna Maris Mortui," *Verbum domini* 30 (1952) 34-35, 101-9
(tr. of 1QJub^{a}, 1Q*19*, 1QMyst)

Molin, G., *Die Söhne des Lichtes: Zeit und Stellung der Handschriften vom Toten Meer* (Vienna/Munich: Herold, 1954)
(tr. of 1QpHab, 1QpMic, 1QS, 1QH, 1QM, 1QMyst, CD)

Moraldi, L., *I manoscritti di Qumrān* (Classici delle religioni; Torino: Unione tipografico--Editrice Torinese, 1971)
(tr. of 1QS, 1QSa, 1QSb, CD, 1QM, 1QH, 11QPs^{a}, 4QpPs37, 3QpIsa, 4QpIsa^{a,b,c,d,e}, 4QpHos^{a,b}, 4QpMic, 1QpMic, 4QpNah, 1QpHab, 4QPBless, 4QFlor, 11QMelch, 4QVisSam (= 4Q*160*), 4QCatena^{a,b}, 4QTanh (= 4Q*176*), 4QTestim, 1QDirMo, 1QapGen, 1QMyst, 1QLitPr, 4QDibHam, 4QOrd, 4QŠirŠabb, 4QPrNab, 4QCryptic, 4QMess aram^{a}, 4QAges, 4QLam (= 4Q*179*), 4QWisdom (= 4Q*185*), 4QWiles, 3Q*15*, 5QJN)
This is the most comprehensive collection of translated texts to date.

Nielsen, E. and B. Otzen, *Dødehavs teksterne: Skrifter fra den jødiske menigheid i Qumran i oversaettelse og med noter* (2d ed.; Copenhagen: G. E. C. Gad, 1959)
(tr. of 1QpHab, 1QpMic, 4QpNah, 1QS, 1QH, 1QM, 1QSa, 1QMyst)

Reicke, B., *Handskrifterna från Qumran (eller ʿAin Feshcha) I-IV* (Symbolae biblicae Upsalienses, 14; Uppsala: Wretman,

1952)
(tr. of 1QpHab, 1QS)

Rosenvasser, A., "Los manuscritos descubiertos en el desierto de Judá," *Davar* (Buenos Aires) 29 (1950) 75-98; 30 (1950) 80-109
(tr. of 1QM, 1QS, 1QH, 1QpHab)

Schreiden, J., *Les énigmes des manuscrits de la Mer Morte* (Wetteren: Editions Cultura, 1961; 2d ed., 1964)
(tr. of 1QpHab, 1QS, 1QSa, CD)

Schubert, K., "Die jüdischen und judenchristlichen Sekten im Lichte des Handschriftenfundes von ʿEn Feščha," *ZKT* 74 (1952) 1-62.
(tr. of 1QpHab, 1QS)

Schubert, K., "Die Texte aus der Sektiererhöhle bei Jericho," *Nötscher-Festschrift* (BBB 1; Bonn: Hanstein, 1950) 224-45.
(tr. of 1QS, 1QH, 1QM)

Sekine, M. (ed.), *Shikai-bunsho* (Tokyo: Yamamoto Shoten, 1963)
(complete translation with notes)

Simotas, P. N., "Ta heurēmata tou Khirbet Qumran," *Nea Sion* 47 (1952) 25-56, 141-46.
(tr. 1QJub[a], 1QMyst, 1QM, 1QH)

Sutcliffe, E. F., *The Monks of Qumran* (Westminster, MD: Newman, 1960)
(tr. of CD, 1QSa, 1QS, 1QpHab, 1QpMic, 4QpNah, 4QpPs37, 1QH, 1QSb, 1QM)

Tyloch, W., *Rekopisy z Qumran ned Morzem Martwym* (Polskie Tow. Religioznawcze, Rozprawy i Materialy 6; Warsaw: Państowe Wyd. Naukowe, 1963)
(tr. of 1QS, 1QSa, 1QM, 1QH, 1QpHab, CD)

Vermes, G., *Les manuscrits du Désert de Juda* (2d ed.; Paris: Desclée, 1954)
(tr. of 1QpHab, 1QS, CD, 1QH, 1QM, 1QMyst, Mur 42, Mur 43)

Vermes, G., *Discovery in the Judean Desert* (New York: Desclée, 1956).

Vermes, G., "Quelques traditions de la communauté de Qumrân d'après les manuscrits de l'Université Hebraïque," *Cahiers sioniens* 9 (1955) 25-58.
(partial tr. of 1QM, 1QH)

Vermes, G., *The Dead Sea Scrolls in English* (Pelican 140205519; Baltimore: Penguin Books, 1962; rev. ed., 1970).
(tr. of 1QS, CD, 1QSa, 1QM, 1QH, 4QDibHam, 1QLitPr, 1QSb, 1QMyst, 4QŠirŠabb, 1QapGen, 4QPBless, 1QDirMo, 4QpIsa[a,b,c,d], 4QpNah, 4QpHos[a], 1QpMic, 4QpNah, 1QpHab, 4QFlor, 4QTestim, 4QOrd)

Vincent, A., *Les manuscrits hébreux du Désert de Juda* (Textes pour l'histoire sacrée; Paris: A. Fayard, 1955).
(tr. of 1QpMic, 1QpHab, 1QS, CD, 1QH, 1QM, 1QJub[a])

Werber, E., *Kršćanstvo prije Krista?* (Zagreb: Liber, 1972)
(partial tr. of 1QS, CD, 1QpHab, 4QpNah, 4QpPs37, 1QM)

9

OUTLINES OF SOME OF THE DEAD SEA SCROLLS

(WITH SELECT BIBLIOGRAPHY)

OUTLINES OF SOME OF THE DEAD SEA SCROLLS

In this section outlines are provided for the Manual of Discipline (1QS), the Damascus Document (CD + 4QD), the Genesis Apocryphon (1QapGen), and the War Scroll (1QM) -- the long sectarian scrolls. No attempt is made to outline the Pesharim, since they follow for the most part the biblical texts on which they are commenting and cannot be divided up topically. The list of their contents and that of other scrolls, such as 11QPs^{a}, given in section 2, are tantamount to outlines and should be consulted for study. The smaller texts, often because of their fragmentary character, do not lend themselves to outlining. The outlines that are provided are followed in some instances by bibliographical references; in others by indications where extensive bibliographies can be found.

SEREK HAY-YAḤAD: THE RULE OF THE COMMUNITY (1QS)

(I)	1:1-15	INTRODUCTION: The Aim and Purpose of the Community
(II)	1:16-3:12	ENTRANCE INTO THE COVENANT
	(A) 1:16-2:18	The Rite for Entrance into the Covenant
	(B) 2:19-25a	The Ceremony for the Assembly of Members
	(C) 2:25b-3:12	The Denunciation of Those Who Refuse to Enter
(III)	3:13-4:26	THE TENETS OF THE COMMUNITY
	(A) 3:13-4:1	The Two Spirits
	(B) 4:2-14	The Activity of the Spirits in Men's Lives
	(C) 4:15-26	The Destiny and End of the Spirits
(IV)	5:1-6:23	THE PURPOSE AND WAY OF LIFE IN THE COMMUNITY
	(A) 5:1-7a	The Statement of the Purpose and the Way
	(B) 5:7b-6:1a	Fidelity to the Way: Avoidance of Outsiders
	(C) 6:1b-8	Rules for Community Life
	(D) 6:8-13a	Rules for a Session of the Members
	(E) 6:13b-23	Rules for Candidates
(V)	6:24-7:25	THE PENAL CODE OF THE COMMUNITY

(VI)	8:1-9:26	THE MODEL, PIONEER COMMUNITY
	(A) 8:1-15a	Constitution and Negative Confession
	(B) 8:15b-9:11	Conduct and Study of the Law until Messianic Times
	(C) 9:12-26	Guidance for the Instructor of the Pioneer Community
(VII)	10:1-11:22	THE HYMN OF THE COMMUNITY
	(A) 10:1-8a	The Creator to be Praised in Times of Worship
	(B) 10:8b-11:2a	Hymn of Praise and Service
	(C) 11:2b-15a	Hymn to God's Righteousness
	(D) 11:15b-22	Hymn of Blessing and Thanksgiving

For the study of the structure of 1QS, see P. Guilbert, "Le plan de la Règle de la Communauté," *RQ* 1 (1958-59) 323-44; A. R. C. Leaney, *The Rule of Qumran and Its Meaning*, 111-13; J. Licht, *The Rule Scroll*, 8-10.

Principal Commentaries or Translations of 1QS
(beyond those listed in section 8 above)

Brownlee, W. H., *The Dead Sea Manual of Discipline: Translation and Notes* (*BASOR* Supplementary Studies, 10-12; New Haven: American Schools of Oriental Research, 1951) (The pioneer translation)

Guilbert, P., "La règle de la Communauté," *Les textes de Qumran traduits et annotés* (ed. J. Carmignac et al.; Paris: Letouzey et Ané) 1 (1961) 9-80.

Lambert, G., "Le Manuel de Discipline de la grotte de Qumrân: Traduction intégrale du 'Manuel de Discipline,'" *NRT* 73 (1951) 938-75 (also incorporated in A. Vincent, *Les manuscrits hébreux du Désert de Juda* [Paris: Fayard, 1955] 120-54)

Leaney, A. R. C., *The Rule of Qumran and Its Meaning* (New Testament Library; London: SCM; Philadelphia: Westminster, 1966)

Licht, J., *M^{e}gillat has-S^{e}rākîm: The Rule Scroll: A Scroll from the Wilderness of Judaea: 1QS, 1QSa, 1QSb: Text, Introduction and Commentary* (Jerusalem: Bialik, 1965) (in modern Hebrew)

Milik, J. T., "Manuale disciplinae," *Verbum domini* 29 (1951) 129-58

Wernberg-Møller, P., *The Manual of Discipline* (STDJ 1; Leiden: Brill, 1957)
(See J. T. Milik's review of this commentary [*RB* 67 (1960) 410-16, esp. pp. 412-16] for variant readings in the different texts of the Serek from Qumran Cave 4)

* * * * *

Of fundamental importance for the study of 1QS is the following article:

Murphy-O'Connor, J., "La genèse littéraire de la Règle de la Communauté," *RB* 76 (1969) 528-49

THE DAMASCUS DOCUMENT (CD AND 4QD)

This tentative outline utilizes Cairo Genizah ms. A and the fragments from Qumran Caves 4, 5, 6 and is arranged according to the indications given by J. T. Milik, *Ten Years*, 151-52. These indications are derived mainly from the copies of $4QD^{b,e}$.

(I) 4Q columns [missing in CD] + CD 1:1-8:21 (= 19:1-20:34) EXHORTATION: GOD'S SAVING PLAN IN HISTORY

- (A) Introductory Columns in 4Q texts
- (B) Meditation on the Lessons of History (CD 1:1-2:1)
- (C) Predestination of the Upright and of the Wicked (2:2-13)
- (D) A Second Meditation on the Lessons of History (2:14-4:12a)
- (E) The Three Nets of Belial (4:12b-6:2a [6Q*15* 1:1-3 = CD 4:19-21; 6Q*15* 2:1-2 = CD 5:13-14; 6Q*15* 3:1-5a = CD 5:18-6:2a])
- (F) The Community of the New Covenant (6:2b-7:9a [6Q*15* 3:5 = CD 6:2b; 6Q*15* 4:1-4 = CD 6:20-7:1. CD 19:1-5a (ms. B) = 7:5b-9a])
- (G) Diverse Fates of Those Who are Faithful to the Covenant and of Those Who are Apostates (7:9b-8:21 [= (ms. B) 19:5b-34])
- (H) Conclusion (ms. B: 19:35-20:34)

(II) 4Q columns [missing in CD] PRESCRIPTIONS

- (A) Cultic Purity of Priests and Sacrifices
- (B) The Law of Diseases (cf. Lev 13:29ff.)
- (C) The Fluxes of Men and Women (Lev 15)
- (D) Laws of Marriage
- (E) Prescriptions Relating to Agricultural Life, Payment of Tithes, Relations with Pagans, Relations between the Sexes; a Prohibition of Magic

(III) 15:1-16:20; 9:1-14:22 CONSTITUTION: LIFE IN THE NEW COVENANT [+ 4Q texts]

- (A) Rules for Entrance into the Covenant and for Oaths (15:1-16:16)
  - (1) The Oath by Which to Swear (15:1-5a)
  - (2) Admission into the Community (15:5b-19 [15:15-17 can be restored as in $4QD^b$; see J. T. Milik, *Ten Years*, 114])
  - (3) Oath on Entering the Covenant (16:1-6a)

(4) The Validity of Oaths (16:6b-12)

(5) Voluntary Gifts (16:13-16)

(B) Regulations within the Community (9:1-10:10a)

(1) Fraternal Correction (9:1-6; 4QD[e] 10 iii ?-20; 9:7-8a [= 5Q*12* 1:2])

(2) Judicial Oaths (9:8b-16a [5Q*12* 1:3-5 = CD 9:8b-10])

(3) Witnesses (9:16b-10:3)

(4) Judges (10:4-10a)

(C) Rites to be Observed in the Community (10:10b-12:18)

(1) Purification with Water (10:10b-13)

(2) Sabbath Regulations (10:14-11:18a)

(3) Sundry Regulations (11:18b-12:11a)

(a) Sacrificial Offerings through an Unclean Intermediary (11:18b-21a)

(b) Entrance into Temple in a State of Uncleanness (11: 21b-23)

(c) Defilement of a Sanctuary (12:1-3 [cf. 6Q*15* 5:1-5; does it belong here?])

(d) Profanation of the Sabbath (12:3b-6a)

(e) Killing or Robbing Pagans (12:6b-8a)

(f) Commerce with Outsiders (12:8b-11a)

(4) Ritual Purity (12:11b-18)

(D) The Organization of the Community (12:19-14:19)

(1) Preamble (12:19-13:2a)

(2) Local Communities (13:2b-7a)

(3) The Overseer of the Camp (13:7b-14:2)

(4) Functionaries in the Community (14:3-12a)

(5) The Works of the Community (14:12b-19)

(E) The Penal Code (14:20-22)

(F) Liturgy for the Feast of the Renewal of the Covenant [4Q columns]

(IV) [4Q columns] CONCLUSION (see J. T. Milik, *RB* 63 [1956] 61)

N.B. Two mss. of CD came from the Cairo Genizah: Ms. A (10th cent.) contains 8 sheets with cols. 1-16; ms. B (12th cent.) contains one sheet with cols. 19-20. The latter coincide roughly with cols. 7

and 8 of ms. A, but the last part of col. 20 corresponds to nothing in ms. A. For an extensive bibliography on CD, see S. Schechter, *Documents of Jewish Sectaries* [with prolegomenon by J. A. Fitzmyer; 2 vols. in one; New York: Ktav, 1970] 25-34)

See further:

Murphy-O'Connor, J., "An Essene Missionary Document? CD II, 14 -- VI, 1," *RB* 77 (1970) 201-29

Murphy-O'Connor, J., "A Literary Analysis of Damascus Document VI, 2 -- VIII, 3," *RB* 78 (1971) 210-32

Murphy-O'Connor, J., "The Critique of the Princes of Judah (CD VIII, 3-19)," *RB* 79 (1972) 200-16

Murphy-O'Connor, J., "A Literary Analysis of Damascus Document XIX, 33 -- XX, 34," *RB* 79 (1972) 544-64

THE GENESIS APOCRYPHON (1QapGen) or THE BOOK OF THE PATRIARCHS

(The beginning of the scroll is lost; see 1Q*20* for some fragments of it)

(I) THE STORY OF NOAH (1QapGen 1:? -- 17:?)

(A) Lamech's Anxiety about the Conception of His Son Noah (2:1-5:?)

(B) Noah and the Flood (6:?-10:?)

(C) God's Covenant with Noah (11:?--)

(D) Noah Divides the Earth among His Sons (16:?-17:?)

(II) THE STORY OF ABRAM (18:? -- ??)

(A) Abram in Ur and Haran (18:?-?)

(B) Abram in Canaan (18:?-19:9)

(1) Abram's Journey to Bethel (19:?-6)

(2) Abram's Journey from Bethel to Hebron (19:7-9)

(C) Abram in Egypt (19:10-20:33)

(1) Abram's Descent to Egypt Because of a Famine (19:10-13)

(2) Abram's Dream on Entering Egypt: The Cedar and the Date-Palm (19:14-23a)

(3) Abram is Visited by Three Nobles of the Pharaoh's Court (19:23b-27)

(4) Sarai's Beauty is Described by the Nobles to Pharaoh Zoan (20:2-8a)

(5) The Pharaoh Carries Off Sarai; Abram's Prayer (20:8b-16a)

(6) God Punishes Pharaoh and All His Household with a Plague (20:16b-21a)

(7) Abram Cures Pharaoh Who Returns Sarai Untouched after Learning Her True Identity (20:21b-31a)

(8) Pharaoh Sends Sarai and Abram from Egypt with Gifts and an Escort (20:31b-33)

(D) Abram in the Promised Land (20:34-21:22)

(1) Abram Returns with Lot to Bethel (20:34-21:4)

(2) Lot Leaves Abram and Goes to Dwell in Sodom (21:5-7)

(3) Abram's Dream: The Promised Land (21:8-14)

(4) Abram Explores the Promised Land (21:15-22)

(E) Abram's Defeat of the Four Invading Kings (21:23-22:26)

(1) Four Kings Invade and Defeat the Five Canaanite Kings (21:23-34a)

(2) Lot is Taken Captive (21:34b-22:5a)

(3) Abram Goes in Pursuit of the Four Kings (22:5b-12a)

(4) The Kings of Sodom and Salem Go out to Meet Abram on His Return from the Defeat (22:12b-26)

(F) Abram's Vision: God Tells Him of His Heir (22:27--?)

(1) Eliezer, His Household Servant, Will Not Inherit Him (22:27-34)

Bibliography on 1QapGen can be found in my commentary: *The Genesis Apocryphon of Qumran Cave I: A Commentary* (Biblica et orientalia, 18; Rome: Biblical Institute, 1966; 2d rev. ed., 18A, 1971).

THE WAR SCROLL (1QM)

- (I) INTRODUCTION (1:1-?)
    - (A) The Rule of the War to Come (1:1-7)
    - (B) The Time Appointed for the Final Carnage (1:8-15)
    - (C) The Annihilation of the Sons of Darkness (1:16-?)
- (II) PREPARATION FOR THE FINAL WAR (1:?-2:14)
    - (A) The Reorganization of Worship to be Carried out during the Struggle (1:?-2:6a)
    - (B) The Gathering for the War (2:6b-9a)
    - (C) The Thirty-Five Years of the Battle and Its Operations (2:9b-14)
- (III) RULES CONCERNING TRUMPETS, STANDARDS, AND SHIELDS IN THE STRUGGLE (2:15-5:2)
    - (A) The Rule for the Trumpets (2:15-3:11)
        - (1) The Sounding of the Trumpets (2:15-3:2a)
        - (2) Inscriptions on the Trumpets (3:2b-11)
    - (B) The Rule for the Standards (3:13-4:17+)
        - (1) Inscriptions on the Standards of the Entire Congregation (3:13-17+)
        - (2) Inscriptions on the Standard of the Clan of Merari (4:1-5)
        - (3) Changes on the Standards of the Levites (4:6-8)
        - (4) Changes on the Standards of the Congregation (4:9-14)
        - (5) Dimensions of the Standards (4:15-17+)
    - (C) The Rule for the Shields (4:?-5:2)
        - (1) ? (4:?-?)
        - (2) Inscriptions on the Shields (4:?-5:2)
- (IV) THE BATTLE-ARRAY AND WEAPONS OF THE INFANTRY (5:3-6:6)
    - (A) The Rule for the Arming and Drawing Up of the Troops (5:3-14)
    - (B) The Battle Array (5:16-6:6)
- (V) THE ARRAY OF THE CAVALRY (6:8-17+)
- (VI) THE RECRUITMENT AND THE AGE OF THE SOLDIERS (6:?-7:7)
- (VII) THE ROLE OF THE PRIESTS AND THE LEVITES IN THE CAMP (7:9-9:9)

(VIII) THE RULE FOR CHANGES IN BATTLE-ARRAY FOR AN ATTACK (9:10-18+)

(IX) THE HIGH PRIEST'S EXHORTATION IN THE BATTLE-LITURGY (9:?-12:18+)

- (A) The Discourse of the High Priest (9:?-10:8a)
- (B) The Prayer of the High Priest (10:8b-12:18+)
  - (1) Praise of God's Power Evidenced in His Deeds (10:8b-11:12)
  - (2) God's Power Will Accomplish New Things (11:13-12:5)
  - (3) The Call of Divine Intervention (12:7-18+)

(X) THE BLESSING UTTERED BY ALL THE LEADERS OF THE COMMUNITY AT VICTORY (12:?-14:1)

- (A) God be Blessed! (12:?-13:3)
- (B) Belial be Cursed! (13:4-6)
- (C) Victory for the Sons of Light Comes from God (13:7-16)
- (D) ? (13:18-14:1)

(XI) THE CEREMONY OF THANKSGIVING (14:2-18+)

- (A) Blessed be God! (14:2-15)
- (B) A Call for Aid (14:16-18+)

(XII) THE LAST BATTLE AGAINST THE KITTIM (14:?-19:13)

- (A) The Beginning of the Battle (14:?-16:9)
  - (1) The Arrival of the Troops (14:?-15:3)
  - (2) The Exhortation Addressed to the First Troop (15:4-16:1)
  - (3) The Combat Engagement of the First Troop (16:3-9)
- (B) The Second Troop (16:11-17:17+)
  - (1) The Coming Forth of the Second Troop (16:11-14)
  - (2) The Exhortation Addressed to the Second Troop (16:15-17:3)
  - (3) The Exhortation to Bravery (17:4-9)
  - (4) The Combat Engagement of the Second Troop (17:10-17+)
- (C) The Third to the Seventh Troops (17:?-18:3a)
- (D) The Destruction of the Kittim (18:3b-6a)
- (E) A Prayer of Thanksgiving (18:6b-19:8)
- (F) The Ceremony after the Battle (19:9-13)

Principal Commentaries or Translations of 1QM
(beyond those listed in section 8 above)

Carmignac, J., *La règle de la guerre des fils de lumière contre les fils de ténèbres: Texte restauré, traduit, commenté* (Paris: Letouzey et Ané, 1958)

Carmignac, J., "La règle de la guerre," *Les textes de Qumran traduits et annotés* (ed. J. Carmignac et al.; Paris: Letouzey et Ané) 1 (1961) 81-125

Dupont-Sommer, A., "Règlement de la guerre des fils de lumière: Traduction et notes," *RHR* 148 (1955) 25-43, 141-80

Jones, R. G., *The Rules for the War of the Sons of Light with the Sons of Darkness* (?: Privately published, 1956)

Jongeling, B., *Le rouleau de la guerre des manuscrits de Qumrân* (Assen: Van Gorcum, 1962)

Ploeg, J. van der, *Le rouleau de la guerre: Traduit et annoté avec une introduction* (STDJ 2; Leiden: Brill, 1959)

Yadin, Y., *M^e^gillat milḥemet b^e^nê 'ôr ûb^e^nê ḥošek* (Jerusalem: Bialik, 1955); *The Scroll of the War of the Sons of Light against the Sons of Darkness* (tr. C. Rabin; Oxford: Oxford University, 1962)

10

SELECT BIBLIOGRAPHY ON SOME TOPICS OF DEAD SEA SCROLLS STUDY

SELECT BIBLIOGRAPHY ON SOME TOPICS OF DEAD SEA SCROLLS STUDY

The purpose of this section is to guide the student to the more important writings on various topics that have become areas of research in the study of the Dead Sea Scrolls. No effort is made here to be exhaustive on any of the topics, since it suffices to list the more important materials, which will of themselves contain references and guides to further literature. In some instances the literature on a topic is more abundant than others; but that is not to be taken as a gauge of the importance of the topic. In some instances the literature has grown about a topic simply because of an extrinsic reason, e.g., the piecemeal fashion in which some of the texts have been published. The areas for special bibliographies here are the following:

I. PALAEOGRAPHY OF THE DEAD SEA SCROLLS

The two most fundamental studies to date are:

Avigad, N., "The Palaeography of the Dead Sea Scrolls and Related Documents," *Aspects of the Dead Sea Scrolls* (Scripta hierosolymitana, 4; Jerusalem: Magnes, 1958) 56-87

Cross, F. M., "The Development of the Jewish Scripts," *The Bible and the Ancient Near East: Essays in Honor of William Foxwell Albright* (Anchor Books A431; Garden City, NY: Doubleday, 1965) 170-264

See further:

Eissfeldt, O., "Ansetzung der Rollen nach paläographischen Kriterien," *TLZ* 74 (1949) 226-28

Birnbaum, S. A., *The Qumrân (Dead Sea) Scrolls and Palaeography* (*BASOR* Supplementary Studies, 13-14; New Haven: American Schools of Oriental Research, 1952)

Cross, F. M., "The Oldest Manuscripts from Qumran," *JBL* 74 (1955) 147-72

Cross, F. M., "Excursus on the Palaeographical Dating of the Copper Document," *Les 'Petites Grottes' de Qumrân* (DJD 3) 217-21

Cross, F. M., "Epigraphic Notes on Hebrew Documents of the Eighth-Sixth Centuries B.C.: II. The Murabbaʿât Papyrus and the Letter Found near Yabneh-Yam," *BASOR* 165 (1962) 34-46

Hanson, R. S., "Paleo-Hebrew Scripts in the Hasmonean Age," *BASOR* 175 (1964) 26-42

II. ARCHAEOLOGY OF THE DEAD SEA SCROLLS

To be noted above all are the following surveys and preliminary or official reports on various caves that have been published to date:

Vaux, R. de, *Archaeology and the Dead Sea Scrolls* (The Schweich Lectures of the British Academy 1959; London: Oxford University, 1973) (This is a revised translation of the original French survey, *L'archéologie et les manuscrits de la Mer Morte* [London: Oxford University, 1961])

Lankester Harding, G. et al., "Archaeological Finds," *Qumran Cave I* (DJD 1) 3-40 (Official report)

Vaux, R. de, "Archéologie," *Les 'Petites Grottes' de Qumrân* (DJD 3) 1-36 (with an appendix by J. T. Milik, "Deux jarres inscrites d'une grotte de Qumrân," pp. 37-41) (Official report)

Vaux, R. de, et al., "Archéologie," *Les grottes de Murabbaʿât* (DJD 2) 1-63 (Official report)

Yadin, Y., *The Finds from the Bar-Kokhba Period in the Cave of Letters* (Judaean Desert Studies, 1; Jerusalem: Israel Exploration Society, 1963) (Official report; a second volume is to present the texts found there)

Aviram, J. et al., "The Expedition to the Judean Desert, 1960," *IEJ* 11 (1961) 3-72

Avigad, N. et al., "The Expedition to the Judean Desert, 1961," *IEJ* 12 (1962) 169-262 (This and the preceding entry are preliminary reports)

Yadin, Y., *Bar Kokhba: The Rediscovery of the Legendary Hero of the Second Jewish Revolt against Rome* (London: Weidenfeld and Nicolson, 1971) (A popular presentation, but which gives much information about the as yet unpublished texts)

Yadin, Y., *Masada: Herod's Fortress and the Zealots' Last Stand* (New York: Random House, 1966) (A popular presentation of the excavation and finds)

Yadin, Y., "The Excavation of Masada -- 1963/64: Preliminary Report," *IEJ* 15 (1965) 1-120

Preliminary Reports on the Qumran Area

These reports have often been superseded by the official ones, but at times they preserve details that become important because of subsequent developments. The most important preliminary reports are the following:

Vaux, R. de, "Post-scriptum: La cachette des manuscrits hébreux," *RB* 56 (1949) 234-37 (Report of the excavation of Qumran Cave 1)

Vaux, R. de, "La grotte des manuscrits hébreux," *RB* 56 (1949) 586-609

Vaux, R. de, "A propos des manuscrits de la Mer Morte," *RB* 57 (1950) 417-29 (De Vaux's initial dating of the pottery, that proved to be too early)

Vaux, R. de, "Fouille au Khirbet Qumrân: Rapport préliminaire," *RB* 60 (1953) 83-106 (Report on the first campaign of excavation at the Qumran community center)

Vaux, R. de, "Exploration de la région de Qumrân," *RB* 60 (1953) 540-61 (Report on the search for further caves, in which the Ecole Biblique and other archaeological institutions in Jerusalem were involved in 1952; see further the two following entries)

Lankester Harding, G., "Khirbet Qumran and Wady Murabbaʿat," *PEQ* 84 (1952) 104-9

Reed, W. L., "The Qumrân Caves Expedition of March, 1952," *BASOR* 135 (1954) 8-13

Vaux, R. de, "Fouilles au Khirbet Qumrân: Rapport préliminaire sur la deuxième campagne," *RB* 61 (1954) 206-36 (Second campaign)

Vaux, R. de, "Chronique archéologique: Khirbet Qumrân," *RB* 61 (1954) 567-68 (Third campaign)

Vaux, R. de, "Chronique archéologique: Khirbet Qumrân," *RB* 63 (1956) 73-74 (Fourth campaign)

Vaux, R. de, "Fouilles de Feshkha: Rapport préliminaire," *RB* 66 (1959) 225-55

Vaux, R. de, "Excavations at ʿAin Feshkha," *ADAJ* 4-5 (1960) 7-11

Vaux, R. de, "Une hachette essénienne," *VT* 9 (1959) 399-407

Other Important Archaeological or Scientific Articles

Burton, D., J. B. Poole, and R. Reed, "A New Approach to the Dating of the Dead Sea Scrolls," *Nature* 184 (No. 4685, 15 August 1959) 533-34

Lapp, P. W., *Palestinian Ceramic Chronology 200 B.C. -- A.D. 70* (New Haven: American Schools of Oriental Research, 1961)

Libby, W. F., "The Accuracy of Radiocarbon Dates," *Antiquity* 37 (1963) 213-19 (reprinted from *Science* 140 [No. 3564, 19 April 1963] 278-80)

Poole, J. B. and R. Reed, "The Preparation of Leather and Parchment by the Dead Sea Scrolls Community," *Technological Culture* 3 (1962) 1-26

Poole, J. B. and R. Reed, "The 'Tannery' of ʿAin Feshkha," *PEQ* 93 (1961) 114-23

Reed, R. and J. B. Poole, "A Study of Some Dead Sea Scroll and Leather Fragments from Cave 4 at Qumran: Part II, Chemical Examination," *Proceedings of the Leeds Philosophical and Literary Society*, Scientific Section 9/6 (1964) 171-82

Sellers, O. R., "Radiocarbon Dating of Cloth from the ʿAin Feshkha Cave," *BASOR* 123 (1951) 24-26

Strobel, A., "Die Wasseranlagen der Ḫirbet Qumrān: Versuch einer Deutung," *ZDPV* 88 (1972) 55-86

Schulz, S., "Chirbet ḳumrān, ʿēn Feschcha und die buḳēʿa: Zugleich ein archäologischer Beitrag zum Felsenaquädukt und zur Strasse durch das wādi ḳumrān," *ZDPV* 76 (1960) 50-72

Stuckenrath, R., "On the Care and Feeding of Radio-carbon Dating," *Archaeology* 18 (1965) 277-81

Zeuner, F. E., "Notes on Qumrân," *PEQ* 92 (1960) 27-36

Controversial Aspects of the Archaeology of Qumran

Vaux, R. de, "Archaeology and the Dead Sea Scrolls," *Antiquity* 37 (1963) 126-27 (Reaction to J. L. Teicher)

Vaux, R. de, "Essenes or Zealots," *NTS* 13 (1966-67) 89-104 (Reaction to G. R. Driver)

Haas, N. and H. Nathan, "Anthropological Survey on the Human Skeletal Remains from Qumran," *RQ* 6 (1967-69) 345-52

Steckoll, S. H., "Preliminary Excavation Report in the Qumran Cemetery," *RQ* 6 (1967-69) 323-44

Steckoll, S. H., "Marginal Notes on the Qumran Excavations," *RQ* 7 (1967-71) 33-44

(On the last entries, note the comments of R. de Vaux, *Archaeology*, 47-48: "The authorities of the Israeli occupation have forbidden this Sherlock Holmes of archaeology [Steckoll] to continue his researches at Qumran.")

III. THE OLD TESTAMENT AT QUMRAN AND MURABBAʿAT

Albright, W. F., "New Light on Early Recensions of the Hebrew Bible," *BASOR* 140 (1955) 27-33

Cross, F. M., "The Contribution of the Qumran Discoveries to the Study of the Biblical Text," *IEJ* 16 (1966) 81-95

Cross, F. M., "The History of the Biblical Text in the Light of Discoveries in the Judaean Desert," *HTR* 57 (1964) 282-99

Cross, F. M., "The Scrolls and the Old Testament," *Christian Century* 73 (1955) 920-22

Cross, F. M., "The Evolution of a Theory of Local Texts," *1971 Proceedings, International Organization for Septuagint and Cognate Studies* (Septuagint and Cognate Studies, 2; Missoula, MT: Society of Biblical Literature, 1972) 108-26

Cross, F. M., *ALQ*, 161-94; *Die antike Bibliothek von Qumran* (see section 4 above), 154-79

Delcor, M., "Zum Psalter von Qumran," *BZ* ns 10 (1966) 15-29

Freedman, D. N., "The Old Testament at Qumran," *NDBA*, 117-26

Freedman, D. N., "The Massoretic Text and the Qumran Scrolls: A Study in Orthography," *Textus* 2 (1962) 87-102

Greenberg, M., "The Stabilization of the Text of the Hebrew Bible, Reviewed in the Light of the Biblical Materials from the Judean Desert," *JAOS* 76 (1956) 157-67

Hoenig, S. B., "The Dead Sea Scrolls and the Bible," *JQR* 48 (1958) 304-6

Howard, G., "Frank Cross and Recensional Critisism [sic]," *VT* 21 (1971) 440-50

Kahle, P., *The Cairo Geniza* (2d ed.; Oxford: Blackwell, 1959)

Kutscher, E. Y., *The Language and Linguistic Background of the Isaiah Scroll (1 Q Isa[a])* (STDJ 6; Leiden: Brill, 1974)

Mansoor, M., "The Massoretic Text in the Light of Qumran," *Congress Volume, Bonn 1962* (VTSup 9; Leiden: Brill, 1963) 305-21

Orlinsky, H. M., "Studies in the St. Mark's Isaiah Scroll," *JBL* 69 (1950) 149-66; *HUCA* 25 (1954) 85-92

Orlinsky, H. M., "Qumran and the Present State of Old Testament Text Studies: The Septuagint Text," *JBL* 78 (1959) 26-33

Orlinsky, H. M., "The Textual Criticism of the Old Testament," *The Bible and the Ancient Near East: Essays in Honor of William Foxwell Albright* (ed. G. E. Wright; Anchor Books A431; Garden City: Doubleday, 1965) 140-69

Purvis, J. D., *The Samaritan Pentateuch and the Origin of the Samaritan Sect* (Harvard Semitic Monographs, 2; Cambridge: Harvard University, 1968)

Rabin, C., "The Dead Sea Scrolls and the History of the O. T. Text," *JTS* ns 6 (1955) 174-82

Roberts, B. J., "The Dead Sea Scrolls and the Old Testament Scriptures," *BJRL* 36 (1953-54) 75-96

Roberts, B. J., "The Old Testament Canon: A Suggestion," *BJRL* 46 (1963) 164-78

Sanders, J. A., "Cave 11 Surprises and the Question of Canon," *McCormick Quarterly* 21 (1968) 1-15 (reprinted in *NDBA*, 101-16)

Sanders, J. A., *DSPS*, 143-55 (Catalogue of pre-Masoretic Psalms); cf. *CBQ* 27 (1965) 114-23

Sanders, J. A., "The Qumran Psalms Scroll (11QPs^{a}) Reviewed," *On Language, Culture, and Religion: In Honor of Eugene A. Nida* (eds. M. Black and W. A. Smalley; The Hague: Mouton, 1974) 79-99

Skehan, P. W., "The Qumran Manuscripts and Textual Criticism," *Volume du congrès, Strasbourg 1956* (VTSup 4; Leiden: Brill, 1957) 148-60

Skehan, P. W., "The Scrolls and the Old Testament Text," *NDBA*, 89-100

Skehan, P. W., "Two Books on Qumran Studies," *CBQ* 21 (1959) 71-78

Skehan, P. W., "Qumran and the Present State of Old Testament Text Studies: The Masoretic Text," *JBL* 78 (1959) 21-25

Skehan, P. W., "The Period of the Biblical Texts from Khirbet Qumrân," *CBQ* 19 (1957) 435-40

Sundberg, A. C., *The Old Testament of the Early Church* (HTS 20; Cambridge: Harvard University, 1964); cf. *HTR* 51 (1958) 205-26; "The 'Old Testament': A Christian Canon," *CBQ* 30 (1968) 143-55

Talmon, S., "Aspects of the Textual Transmission of the Bible in the Light of Qumran Manuscripts," *Textus* 4 (1964) 95-132

Talmon, S., "The Old Testament Text," *Cambridge History of the Bible* (eds. P. R. Ackroyd and C. F. Evans; Cambridge: Cambridge University) 1 (1970) 159-99

IV. OLD TESTAMENT INTERPRETATION IN QUMRAN LITERATURE

Betz, O., *Offenbarung und Schriftforschung in der Qumransekte* (Tübingen: Mohr, 1960)

Brownlee, W. H., "Biblical Interpretation among the Sectaries of the Dead Sea Scrolls," *BA* 14 (1951) 54-76

Bruce, F. F., *Biblical Exegesis in the Qumran Texts* (Grand Rapids: Eerdmans, 1959)

Fitzmyer, J. A., "The Use of Explicit Old Testament Quotations in Qumran Literature and in the New Testament," *NTS* 7 (1960-61) 297-333; revised form, *ESBNT*, 3-58

Gottstein, M. H., "Bible Quotations in the Sectarian Dead Sea Scrolls," *VT* 3 (1953) 79-82

Osswald, E., "Zur Hermeneutik des Habakuk-Kommentar," *ZAW* 68 (1956) 243-56

Ploeg, J. van der, "Bijbelverklaring te Qumrân," *Mededelingen der koninklijke Akademie van Wetenschappen*, Afd. Letterkunde, nieuwe reeks, deel 23, No. 8 (1960) 207-29

Roth, C., "The Subject Matter of Qumran Exegesis," *VT* 10 (1960) 51-65

Schwarz, O. J. R., *Der erste Teil der Damaskusschrift und das Alte Testament* (Diest: Lichtland, 1965)

Talmon, S., "DSIa as a Witness to Ancient Exegesis of the Book of Isaiah," *ASTI* 1 (1962) 62-72

Trever, J. C., "The Qumran Covenanters and Their Use of Scripture," *Personalist* 39 (1958) 127-38

Vermes, G., "A propos des commentaires bibliques découverts à Qumrân," *RHPR* 33 (1955) 95-102

Vermes, G., *Scripture and Tradition in Judaism: Haggadic Studies* (Studia postbiblica, 4; Leiden: Brill, 1961)

Vermes, G., "The Qumran Interpretation of Scripture in Its Historical Setting," *ALUOS* 6 (1966-68) 85-97

Waard, J. de, *A Comparative Study of the Old Testament Text in the Dead Sea Scrolls and in the New Testament* (STDJ 4; Leiden: Brill, 1965)

Wernberg-Møller, P., "Some Reflections on the Biblical Material in the Manual of Discipline," *Studia theologica* 9 (1955) 40-66

Wieder, N., "The Dead Sea Scrolls Type of Biblical Exegesis among the Karaites," *Between East and West* (1958) 75-106

V. QUMRAN THEOLOGY

For articles on various aspects of Qumran theology or religion, see the topical bibliographies of W. S. LaSor and B. Jongeling and the yearly bibliography of P. Nober (see section 3 above), as well as *New Testament Abstracts* (ed. D. J. Harrington; Cambridge: Weston College School of Theology [3 times a year]) and the *Internazionale Zeitschriftenschau für Bibelwissenschaft und Grenzgebiete* (ed. F. Stier; Düsseldorf: Patmos [issued once a year]). Listed below are merely the more important books on the general topic.

Betz, O., *Der Paraklet: Fürsprecher im häretischen Spätjudentum, im Johannesevangelium und in neu gefundenen gnostischen Schriften* (Leiden: Brill, 1963)

Denis, A.-M., *Les thèmes de connaissance dans le Document de Damas* (Studia hellenistica, 15; Louvain: Publications universitaires, 1967)

Huppenbauer, H. W., *Der Mensch zwischen zwei Welten: Der Dualismus der Texte von Qumran (Höhle I) und der Damaskusfragmente: Ein Beitrag zur Vorgeschichte des Evangeliums* (Zürich: Zwingli, 1959)

Jeremias, G., *Der Lehrer der Gerechtigkeit* (Göttingen: Vandenhoeck & Ruprecht, 1963)

Jeremias, J., *Die theologische Bedeutung der Funde am Toten Meer* (Göttingen: Vandenhoeck & Ruprecht, 1962) (translated as "Qumrân et la théologie," *NRT* 85 [1963] 674-90)

Klinzing, G., *Die Umdeutung des Kultus in der Qumrangemeinde und im Neuen Testament* (Studien zur Umwelt des Neuen Testaments, 7; Göttingen: Vandenhoeck & Ruprecht, 1971)

Nötscher, F., *Gotteswege und Menschenwege in der Bibel und in Qumran* (BBB 15; Bonn: Hanstein, 1958)

Nötscher, F., *Zur theologischen Terminologie der Qumran-Texte* (BBB 10; Bonn: Hanstein, 1956)

Osten-Sacken, P. von der, *Gott und Belial: Traditionsgeschichtliche Untersuchungen zum Dualismus in den Texten aus Qumran* (Studien zur Umwelt des Neuen Testaments, 6; Göttingen: Vandenhoeck & Ruprecht, 1969)

Ringgren, H., *The Faith of Qumran: Theology of the Dead Sea Scrolls* (tr. E. T. Sander; Philadelphia: Fortress, 1963)

Schubert, K., *Die Gemeinde vom Toten Meer: Ihre Entstehung und ihre Lehren* (Munich/Basel: E. Reinhardt, 1958)

Strobel, A., *Untersuchungen zum eschatologischen Verzögerungsproblem auf Grund der spätjüdisch-urchristlichen Geschichte von Habakuk 2:2ff.* (Novum Testamentum Sup., 2; Leiden: Brill, 1961)

VI. QUMRAN MESSIANISM

Beasley-Murray, G. R., "The Two Messiahs in the Testaments of the Twelve Patriarchs," *JTS* 48 (1947) 1-12

Black, M., "The Messiah of the Testament of Levi XVIII," *ExpT* 60 (1948-49) 321-22; 61 (1949-50) 157-58

Black, M., "Messianic Doctrine in the Qumran Scrolls," *Studia patristica 1* (= TU 63; eds. K. Aland and F. L. Cross; Berlin: Akademie-V., 1957), 1. 441-59

Brown, R. E., "The Messianism of Qumran," *CBQ* 19 (1957) 53-82

Brown, R. E., "The Teacher of Righteousness and the Messiah(s)," *The Scrolls and Christianity* (ed. M. Black; SPCK Theological Collections, 11; London: S.P.C.K., 1969) 37-44, 109-12

Brown, R. E., "J. Starcky's Theory of Qumran Messianic Development," *CBQ* 28 (1966) 51-57

Brownlee, W. H., "Messianic Motifs of Qumran and the New Testament," *NTS* 3 (1956-57) 12-30, 195-210

Burrows, M., "The Messiahs of Aaron and Israel (DSD IX, 11)" *ATR* 34 (1952) 202-6

Caquot, A., "Ben Sira et le messianisme," *Semitica* 16 (1966) 43-68

Croatto, J. S., "De messianismo qumranico," *Verbum domini* 35 (1957) 279-86, 344-60

Deichgräber, R., "Zur Messiaserwartung der Damaskusschrift," *ZAW* 78 (1966) 333-43

Delcor, M., "Un psaume messianique de Qumrân," *Mélanges bibliques rédigés en l'honneur de André Robert* (Paris: Bloud et Gay, 1957) 334-40

Ehrlich, E. L., "Ein Beitrag zur Messiaslehre der Qumransekte," *ZAW* 68 (1956) 234-43

Fitzmyer, J. A., "The Aramaic 'Elect of God' Text from Qumran Cave 4," *CBQ* 27 (1965) 348-72; slightly revised in *ESBNT*, 127-60

Fritsch, C. T., "The So-called 'Priestly Messiah' of the Essenes," *JEOL* 6 (1959-66) 69-72

Giblet, J., "Prophétisme et attente d'un messie prophète dans l'ancien Judaïsme," *L'attente du Messie* (RechBib 1; ed. B. Rigaux; Bruges: Desclée de Brouwer, 1958) 85-130

Gnilka, J., "Bräutigam -- spätjüdisches Messiasprädikat?" *Trierer theologische Zeitschrift* 69 (1960) 298-301

Gnilka, J., "Die Erwartung des messianischen Hohenpriesters in den Schriften von Qumran und im Neuen Testament," *RQ* 2 (1959-60) 395-426

Gordis, R., "The 'Begotten' Messiah in the Qumran Scrolls," *VT* 7 (1957) 191-94

Greig, J. C. G., "Gospel Messianism and the Qumran Use of Prophecy," *Studia evangelica* 1 (= TU 73; Berlin: Akademie-V., 1959) 593-99

Grelot, P., "Le messie dans les apocryphes de l'Ancien Testament," *La venue du Messie: Messianisme et eschatologie* (RechBib 6; Bruges: Desclée de Brouwer, 1962) 19-50

Grundmann, W., "Die Frage nach der Gottessohnschaft des Messias im Lichte von Qumran," *Bibel und Qumran: Beiträge zur Erforschung der Beziehungen zwischen Bibel- und Qumranwissenschaft: Hans Bardtke zum 22. 9. 1966* (Berlin: Evangelische Haupt-Bibelgesellschaft, 1968) 86-111

Grundmann, W., F. Hesse, M. de Jonge, and A. S. van der Woude, "Χρίω, Χριστός...," *TDNT* 9 (1974) 493-580, esp. pp. 509-20

Héring, J., "Encore le messianisme dans les écrits de Qoumran," *RHPR* 41 (1961) 160-62

Higgins, A. J. B., "Jewish Messianic Belief in Justin Martyr's *Dialogue with Trypho*," *Novum Testamentum* 9 (1967) 298-305

Higgins, A. J. B., "Priest and Messiah," *VT* 3 (1953) 321-36

Higgins, A. J. B., "The Priestly Messiah," *NTS* 13 (1966-67) 211-39

Jonge, M. de, "Jewish Expectations about the 'Messiah' According to the Fourth Gospel," *NTS* 19 (1972-73) 246-70

Jonge, M. de, "The Use of the Word 'Anointed' in the Time of Jesus," *Novum Testamentum* 8 (1966) 132-48

Kuhn, K. G., "Die beiden Messias Aarons und Israels," *NTS* 1 (1954-55) 168-79; translated and adapted in K. Stendahl (ed.), *The Scrolls and the New Testament* (see section 10/VI above) 54-64

Kuhn, K. G., "Die beiden Messias in den Qumrantexten und die Messiasvorstellung in der rabbinischen Literatur," *ZAW* 70 (1958) 200-8

LaSor, W. S., "'The Messiahs of Aaron and Israel,'" *VT* 6 (1956) 425-29

LaSor, W. S., "The Messianic Idea in Qumran," *Studies Presented to A. A. Neuman* (Leiden: Brill, 1962) 343-64

Laurin, R. B., "The Problem of Two Messiahs in the Qumran Scrolls," *RQ* 4 (1963-64) 39-52

Liver, J., "The Doctrine of the Two Messiahs in the Sectarian Literature in the Time of the Second Commonwealth," *HTR* 52 (1959) 149-85

Lohse, E., "Der König aus Davids Geschlecht: Bemerkungen zur messianischen Erwartung der Synagoge," *Abraham unser Vater* (Festschrift O. Michel; Leiden: Brill, 1963) 337-45

Mariès, L., "Le Messie issu de Lévi chez Hippolyte de Rome," *Mélanges J. Lebreton* (*Recherches de science religieuse* 39/1 [1951]) 385-88

Pearce Higgins, A. G. McL., "A Few Thoughts on the Dead Sea Scrolls," *Modern Churchman* 13 (1970) 198-201

Priest, J. F., "Mebaqqer, Paqid, and the Messiah," *JBL* 81 (1962) 55-61

Priest, J. F., "The Messiah and the Meal in 1QSa," *JBL* 82 (1963) 95-100

Prigent, P., "Quelques testimonia messianiques: Leur histoire littéraire de Qoumrân aux Pères de l'église," *TZ* 15 (1959) 419-30

Ragot, A., "Messie essénien et messie chrétien," *Cahiers du cercle Ernest Renan* 37 (1963) 1-10

Rivkin, E., "The Meaning of Messiah in Jewish Thought," *Union Seminary Quarterly Review* 26 (1971) 383-406

Sabbe, M., "Het thema van de Messias, profeet zoals Mozes," *Collationes brugenses* 50 (1954) 148-65

Schubert, K., "Der alttestamentliche Hintergrund der Vorstellung von den beiden Messiassen im Schrifttum von Chirbet Qumran," *Judaica* 12 (1956) 24-28

Schubert, K., "Die Messiaslehre in den Testamenten der 12 Patriarchen im Lichte der Texte von Chirbet Qumran," *Akten des 24. internationalen Orientalisten-Kongresses München 28. August bis 4. September 1957* (Wiesbaden: F. Steiner, 1959) 197-98

Schubert, K., "Die Messiaslehre in den Texten von Chirbet Qumran," *Biblische Zeitschrift* ns 1 (1957) 177-97

Schubert, K., "Zwei Messiasse aus dem Regelbuch von Chirbet Qumran," *Judaica* 11 (1955) 216-35

Segert, S., "Der Messias nach neueren Auffassungen," *Communio viatorum* 2 (1959) 343-53

Silberman, L. H., "The Two 'Messiahs' of the Manual of Discipline," *VT* 5 (1955) 77-82

Smith, M., "'God's Begetting the Messiah' in 1QSa," *NTS* 5 (1958-59) 218-24

Smith, M., "What Is Implied by the Variety of Messianic Figures?" *JBL* 78 (1959) 66-72

Smyth, K., "The Dead Sea Scrolls and the Messiah," *Studies* 45 (1956) 1-14

Starcky, J., "Les quatre étapes du messianisme à Qumran," *RB* 70 (1963) 481-505

Stefaniak, L., "Messianische oder eschatologische Erwartungen in der Qumransekte?" *Neutestamentliche Aufsätze: Festschrift J. Schmid* (Regensburg: Pustet, 1962) 294-302

Villalón, J. R., "Sources vétéro-testamentaires de la doctrine des deux Messies," *RQ* 8 (1972-75) 53-63

Wcela, E. A., "The Messiah(s) of Qumrân," *CBQ* 26 (1964) 340-49

Wieder, N., "The Doctrine of the Two Messiahs among the Karaites," *JJS* 6 (1955) 14-25

Winter, P., "The Holy Messiah," *ZNW* 50 (1959) 275

Woude, A. S. van der, *Die messianischen Vorstellungen der Gemeinde von Qumran* (Studia semitica neerlandica, 3; Assen: Van Gorcum, 1957)

Woude, A. S. van der, "Le Maître de Justice et les deux messies de la communauté de Qumrân," *La secte de Qumrân et les origines chrétiennes* (RechBib 4; Bruges: Desclée de Brouwer, 1959) 121-34

VII. THE NEW TESTAMENT AT QUMRAN ?

This issue has been raised by the writings of José O'Callaghan apropos of the Greek fragments of Qumran Cave 7. Though most scholars have been extremely skeptical about the claims that he has been making --and rightly so--the issue cannot yet be simply dismissed. He has not yet proved his case, and it seems most likely that the frs. *7Q3-18* are nothing more than copies of some Old Greek translation of the OT. The titles that follow are intended simply to give students access to the material that he has published and to the reactions of noted NT scholars. Favorable reactions to the claims have come only from uncritical sources.

The Writings of José O'Callaghan

"¿Papiros neotestamentarios en la cueva 7 de Qumrān?" *Bib* 53 (1972) 91-100 (Engl. tr. by W. L. Holladay, "New Testament Papyri in Qumrân Cave 7?" Supplement to *JBL* 91/2 [1972] 1-14)

"Tres probables papiros neotestamentarios en la cueva 7 de Qumrān," *SP* 11 (1972) 83-89

"¿1 Tim 3,16; 4,1.3 en 7Q4?" *Bib* 53 (1972) 362-67

"¿Un fragmento del Ev. de S. Marcos en el papiro 5 de la cueva 7 de Qumrān?" *Arbor* 81/316 (1972) 429-31

"Die griechischen Papyri aus der Höhle 7 von Qumran," *Bibel und Liturgie* 45 (1972) 121-22

"Sobre los papiros de la cueva 7 de Qumrān," *Boletín de la asociación española de orientalistas* 8 (1972) 205-6

"Les papyrus de la grotte 7 de Qumrân," *NRT* 95 (1973) 188-95

"El ordenador, 7Q5 y Homero," *SP* 12 (1973) 73-79

"La identificación de papiros literarios (bíblicos)," *SP* 12 (1973) 91-100

"Notas sobre 7Q tomadas en el 'Rockefeller Museum' de Jerusalén," *Bib* 53 (1972) 517-33

"El cambio δ > τ en los papiros bíblicos," *Bib* 54 (1973) 415-16

Los papiros griegos de la cueva 7 de Qumrân (BAC 353; Madrid: Editorial católica, 1974)

"El ordenador, 7Q5 y los autores griegos (Apolonio de Rodas, Aristóteles, Lisias)," *SP* 13 (1974) 21-29

"Sobre la identificación de 7Q4," *SP* 13 (1974) 45-55

"Nota sobre 7Q4 y 7Q5," *SP* 13 (1974) 61-63

"¿El texto de 7Q5 es Tuc. I 41,2?" *SP* 13 (1974) 125 (+ pl.) [Tuc. = Thucydides]

Secondary Literature on O'Callaghan's Publications

Could One Small Fragment Shake the World? (= *Eternity* 23/6 [Philadelphia: Evangelical Foundation, 1972] 1-14)

Aland, K., "Neue neutestamentliche Papyri? Ein Nachwort zu den angeblichen Entdeckungen von Prof. O'Callaghan," *Bibel und Kirche* 28 (1973) 19-20

Aland, K., "Neue neutestamentliche Papyri III," *NTS* 20 (1973-74) 357-81

Baillet, M., "Les manuscrits de la grotte 7 de Qumrân et le Nouveau Testament," *Bib* 53 (1972) 508-16; 54 (1973) 340-50

Bartina, S., "La cueva séptima de Qumrán y sus papiros neotestamentarios," *EstEcl* 48 (1973) 87-91

Bartina, S., "Identificación de papiros neotestamentarios en la cueva 7 de Qumrân," *Cultura bíblica* 29 (1972) 195-206

Benoit, P., "Note sur les fragments grecs de la grotte 7 de Qumrân," *RB* 79 (1972) 321-24

Benoit, P., "Nouvelle note sur les fragments grecs de la grotte 7 de Qumrân," *RB* 80 (1973) 5-12

Bernardi, J., "L'évangile de Saint Marc et la grotte 7 de Qumrân," *Etudes théologiques et religieuses* 47 (1972) 453-56

Briend, J., "La grotte 7 de Qumran et le Nouveau Testament," *Bibel et terre sainte* 143 (1972) 24

Duplacy, J., "Bulletin de critique textuelle du Nouveau Testament, V (1ère partie)," *Bib* 54 (1973) 79-114, esp. pp. 92-93

Estrada, D., "On the Latest Identification of New Testament Documents," *WTJ* 34 (1972) 109-17

Fee, G., "Some Dissenting Notes on 7Q5 = Mark 6:52-53," *JBL* 92 (1973) 109-12

Fisher, E., "New Testament Documents among the Dead Sea Scrolls," *The Bible Today* 61 (1972) 835-41

Fitzmyer, J. A., "A Qumran Fragment of Mark?" *America* 126/25 (No. 3265; 24 June 1972) 647-50

Garnet, P., "O'Callaghan's Fragments: Our Earliest New Testament Texts?" *EvQ* 45 (1973) 6-12

Ghiberti, G., "Dobbiamo anticipare la data di composizione dei Vangeli?" *Parole di vita* 17 (1972) 303-6

Hemer, C. J., "New Testament Fragments at Qumran?" *Tyndale Bulletin* 23 (1972) 125-28

Legrand, L., "The New Testament at Qumran?" *Indian Ecclesiastical Studies* 11 (1972) 157-66

Martini, C., "Note sui papiri della grotta 7 di Qumrân," *Bib* 53 (1972) 101-4 (Engl. tr. by W. L. Holladay, "Notes on the Papyri of Qumrân Cave 7," Supplement to *JBL* 91/2 [1972] 15-20)

Martini, C., "Testi neotestamentari tra i manoscritti del deserto di Giuda?" *Civiltà cattolica* 123 (1972) 156-58; cf. *Rocca* (Assisi) 11 (1 June 1972) 26-27

Mejía, J., "Un problema bíblico: La antigüedad del Nuevo Testamento," *Criterio* (Buenos Aires) 45 (1972) 270-73

Noack, B., "Note om påståede stumper af det Nye Testamente i Qumran," *DTT* 36 (1973) 152-55

[Orchard, B.,], "A Fragment of St. Mark's Gospel Dating from before AD 50?" *Biblical Apostolate* (Rome) 6 (1972) 5-6

Parker, P., "7 Q 5: Enthält das Papyrusfragment 5 aus der Höhle 7 von Qumran einen Markustext?" *Erbe und Auftrag* 48 (1972) 467-69

Reicke, B., "Fragmente neutestamentlicher Papyri bei Qumrân?" *TZ* 28 (1972) 304

Roberts, C. H., "On Some Presumed Papyrus Fragments of the New Testament from Qumran," *JTS* ns 23 (1972) 446-47

Roberts, C. H., "A Papyrus Fragment," *London Times*, 7 April 1972, p. 15

Sabourin, L., "Un papyrus de Marc à Qumran?" *Bulletin de théologie biblique* 2 (1972) 309-13; Engl. tr.: "A Fragment of Mark at Qumran?" *Biblical Theology Bulletin* 2 (1972) 308-12; cf. *Selecciones de Teologia* 12/45 (1972) 66-67

Sacchi, P., "Scoperta di frammenti neotestamentari in una grotta di Qumran," *Rivista di storia e letteratura religiosa* 8 (1972) 429-31

Salvoni, F., "Qumran e le Pastorali," *Ricerche bibliche e religiose* 7 (1972) 147-48

Spottorno, M. V., "Nota sobre los papiros de la cueva 7 de Qumran," *Estudios clásicos* 15 (1972) 261-63

Urbán, A. C., "Observaciones sobre ciertos papiros de la cueva 7 de Qumran," *RQ* 8 (1972-74) 233-51

Vardaman, J., "The Earliest Fragments of the New Testament?" *ExpT* 83 (1971-72) 374-76

Vardaman, J., "The Gospel of Mark and 'The Scrolls,'" *Christianity Today* 17 (1973) 1284-87

Vermes, G., "A Papyrus Fragment," *London Times*, 1 April 1972, p. 15

Vogt, E., "Entdeckung neutestamentlicher Texte beim Toten Meer?" *Orientierung* 36 (1972) 138-40

Voulgaris, C. S., "Nea heurēmata apospasmatōn bibliōn tēs Kainēs Diathēkēs," *Theologia* (Athens) 43 (1972) 458-63

White, W., Jr., "A Layman's Guide to O'Callaghan's Discovery," *Eternity* 23/6 (1972) 27-31

White, W., Jr., "O'Callaghan's Identifications: Confirmation and Its Consequences," *WTJ* 35 (1972) 15-20

White, W., Jr., "Notes on the Papyrus Fragments from Cave 7 at Qumran," *WTJ* 35 (1972-73) 221-26

Zurro, E., "El importante hallazgo del P. O'Callaghan," *Vida nueva* 828 (15 April 1972) 22-25

Zurro, E., "El P. Alonso Schökel comenta el hallazgo escrituristico de O'Callaghan," *Vida neuva* 828 (15 April 1972) 26-29

VIII. THE QUMRAN SCROLLS AND THE NEW TESTAMENT

Much has been written about the bearing of the Qumran texts on books of the NT. No attempt is being made to cover that relationship here in a comprehensive way. For articles on the various aspects of the relationship between these two bodies of literature, one should consult the topical bibliographies of W. S. LaSor and B. Jongeling and the yearly bibliography of P. Nober (see section 3 above), as well as *New Testament Abstracts* (ed. D. J. Harrington; Cambridge: Weston College School of Theology [3 times a year]) and the *Internazionale Zeitschriftenschau für Bibelwissenschaft und Grenzgebiete* (ed. F. Stier; Düsseldorf: Patmos [issued once a year]). Listed below are merely the more important books on the general topic and on two specific areas of it (in the latter cases, some of the more important articles are included).

Black, M., *The Scrolls and Christian Origins: Studies in the Jewish Background of the New Testament* (New York: Scribner, 1961)

Black, M. (ed.), *The Scrolls and Christianity* (SPCK Theological Collections, 11; London: S.P.C.K., 1969)

Braun, H., *Qumran und das Neue Testament* (2 vols.; Tübingen: Mohr, 1966)
(Vol. 1 is a reprinting of articles that appeared in *Theologische Rundschau* 28-30 (1962-64) and constituted an analytical survey of literature on Qumran in the preceding ten years; vol. 2 is a synthetic approach to many topics related to the NT. This is a fundamental, indispensable work.)

Carmignac, J., *Christ and the Teacher of Righteousness: The Evidence of the Dead Sea Scrolls* (Baltimore: Helicon, 1962)

Daniélou, J., *The Dead Sea Scrolls and Primitive Christianity* (2d ed.; Baltimore: Helicon, 1963); revised French edition, *Les manuscrits de la Mer Morte et les origines du christianisme* (Paris: Editions de l'Orante, 1974)

Fitzmyer, J. A., *ESBNT*, 3-89, 127-60, 187-354, 435-80

Graystone, G., *The Dead Sea Scrolls and the Originality of Christ* (New York: Sheed and Ward, 1956)

Jeremias, J., *Die theologische Bedeutung der Funde am Toten Meer* (2d ed.; Göttingen: Vandenhoeck & Ruprecht, 1962)

LaSor, W. S., *The Dead Sea Scrolls and the New Testament* (Grand Rapids: Eerdmans, 1972)

Mowry, L., *The Dead Sea Scrolls and the Early Church* (Chicago: University of Chicago, 1962)

Praag, H. van (ed.), *Studies on the Jewish Background of the New Testament* (Assen: Van Gorcum, 1969)

Rowley, H. H., *The Dead Sea Scrolls and the New Testament* (London: S.P.C.K., 1957)

Rowley, H. H., "The Qumran Sect and Christian Origins," *Bulletin of the John Rylands Library* 44 (1961) 119-56; reprinted separately (Manchester: J. R. Library, 1961)

Schelkle, K. H., *Die Gemeinde von Qumran und die Kirche des Neuen Testaments* (Die Welt der Bibel; 2d ed.; Düsseldorf: Patmos, 1965)

Stauffer, E., *Jesus und die Wüstengemeinde am Toten Meer* (Calwer Hefte, 9; 2d ed.; Stuttgart: Calwer V., 1960)

Stendahl, K. (ed.), *The Scrolls and the New Testament* (New York: Harper, 1957)

Ploeg, J. van der (ed.), *La secte de Qumrân et les origines du Christianisme* (RechBib 4; Bruges: Desclée de Brouwer, 1959)

A. *Qumran Literature and Pauline Writings*

In addition to the literature surveyed in H. Braun, *Qumran und das Neue Testament* (see above), 1. 169-240; 2. 165-80, and that collected in K. Stendahl (ed.), *The Scrolls and the New Testament*, 65-113, 157-82, one should note in particular the following title:

Murphy-O'Connor, J. (ed.), *Paul and Qumran: Studies in New Testament Exegesis* (Chicago: Priory, 1968)

See further:

Braun, H., "Römer 7,7-25 und das Selbstverständnis des Qumranfrommen," *ZTK* 56 (1959) 1-18

Brown, R. E., *The Semitic Background of the Term "Mystery" in the New Testament* (Facet Books, Biblical Series, 21; Philadelphia: Fortress, 1968)

Cadbury, H. J., "A Qumran Parallel to Paul," *HTR* 51 (1958) 1-2; cf. J. A. Fitzmyer, *NTS* 4 (1957-58) 48-58; *ESBNT*, 187-204

Fitzmyer, J. A., "Qumrân and the Interpolated Paragraph in 2 Cor 6,14-7,1," *CBQ* 23 (1961) 271-80; slightly revised, *ESBNT*, 205-17

Grundmann, W., "Der Lehrer der Gerechtigkeit von Qumran und die Frage nach der Glaubensgerechtigkeit in der Theologie des Apostels Paulus," *RQ* 2 (1959-60) 237-59

Kertelge, K., *"Rechtfertigung" bei Paulus: Studien zur Struktur und zum Bedeutungsgehalt des paulinischen Rechtfertigungsbegriffs* (Neutestamentliche Abhandlungen, ns 3; 2d ed.; Münster: Aschendorff, 1967)

Kuhn, K.-G., "Der Epheserbrief im Lichte der Qumrantexte," *NTS* 7 (1960-61) 334-46

Osborne, R. E., "Did Paul Go to Qumran?" *Canadian Journal of Theology* 10 (1964) 15-24

Penna, A., "L'elezione nella lettera ai Romani e nei testi di Qumran," *Divinitas* 2 (1958) 597-614

Penna, A., "Testi d'Isaia in S. Paolo," *Revista biblica* 5 (1957) 25-30, 163-79

Rad, G. von, "Die Vorgeschichte der Gattung von 1. Kor. 13,4-7," *Festschrift Albrecht Alt zum 70. Geburtstag* (Beiträge zur historischen Theologie, 16; Tübingen: Mohr, 1953) 153-68

Sanders, J. A., "Dissenting Deities and Philippians 2:1-11," *JBL* 88 (1969) 279-90

Sanders, J. A., "Habakkuk in Qumran, Paul, and the Old Testament," *Journal of Religion* 39 (1959) 232-44

Schneider, G., "Die Idee der Neuschöpfung beim Apostel Paulus und ihr religionsgeschichtlicher Hintergrund," *Trierer theologische Zeitschrift* 68 (1959) 257-70

Schulz, S., "Zur Rechtfertigung aus Gnaden in Qumran und bei Paulus: Zugleich ein Beitrag zur Form- und Überlieferungsgeschichte der Qumrantexte," *ZTK* 56 (1959) 155-85

Schweizer, E., "Zur Interpretation des Römerbriefes," *EvT* 22 (1962) 105-7

Schweizer, E., "Röm. 1,3f. und der Gegensatz von Fleisch und Geist vor und bei Paulus," *EvT* 12 (1952-53) 563-71

Stendahl, K., "Hate, Non-Retaliation, and Love (1QS X, 17-20 and Rom. 12:19-21)," *HTR* 55 (1962) 343-55

Stuhlmacher, P., *Gerechtigkeit Gottes bei Paulus* (FRLANT 87; Göttingen: Vandenhoeck & Ruprecht, 1965)

Thierry, J. J., "Der Dorn im Fleische (2 Kor. XII 7-9)," *Novum Testamentum* 5 (1962) 301-10

Wibbing, S., *Die Tugend- und Lasterkataloge im Neuen Testament und ihre Traditionsgeschichte unter besonderer Berücksichtigung der Qumrantexte* (BZNW 25; Berlin: Töpelmann, 1959)

Wood, J. E., "Pauline Studies and the Dead Sea Scrolls," *ExpT* 78 (1966-67) 308-10

Yamauchi, E., "Qumran and Colossae," *Bibliotheca sacra* 121 (1964) 141-52

Zedda, S., "Il carattere gnostico e giudaico dell'errore colossese nella luce dei manoscritti del Mar Morto," *Rivista biblica* 5 (1957) 31-56

B. *Qumran Literature and Johannine Writings*

Again in addition to the literature surveyed in H. Braun, *Qumran und das Neue Testament* (see above), 1. 96-138, 290-326; 2. 118-44, and that collected in K. Stendahl (ed.), *The Scrolls and the New Testament*, 183-207, one should note in particular the following title:

Charlesworth, J. H. (ed.), *John and Qumran* (London: Chapman, 1972)

See further:

Baumbach, G., *Qumrān und das Johannes-Evangelium* (Aufsätze und Vorträge zur Theologie und Religionswissenschaft, 6; Berlin: Evangelische Verlagsanstalt, 1957)

Böcher, O., *Der johanneische Dualismus im Zusammenhang des nachbiblischen Judentums* (Gütersloh: Mohn, 1965)

Boismard, M.-E., "Qumrán y los escritos de S. Juan," *Cultura bíblica* 12 (1955) 250-64

Braun, F.-M., "L'arrière-fond judaïque du quatrième évangile et la communauté de l'alliance," *RB* 62 (1955) 5-44

Brown, R. E., "John and Qumran," *The Gospel According to John* (Anchor Bible, 29; Garden City: Doubleday, 1966) lxii-lxvi

Cullmann, O., "Secte de Qumran, Hellénistes des Actes et Quatrième Evangile," *Les manuscrits de la Mer Morte: Colloque de Strasbourg 25-27 mai 1955* (Paris: Presses universitaires de France, 1957) 61-74, 135-36

Cullmann, O., "L'opposition contre le Temple de Jérusalem, motif commun de la théologie johannique et du monde ambiant," *NTS* 5 (1958-59) 157-73

Kuhn, K. G., "Johannesevangelium und Qumrantexte," *Neotestamentica et patristica* (Festschrift O. Cullmann; Leiden: Brill, 1962) 111-22

Lákatos, E., "El cuarto evangelio y los descubrimientos de Qumran," *Revista de teologia* 21 (1956) 67-77

Mowry, L., "The Dead Sea Scrolls and the Gospel of John," *BA* 17 (1954) 78-97

Roloff, J., "Der johanneische 'Lieblingsjünger' und der Lehrer der Gerechtigkeit," *NTS* 15 (1968-69) 129-51

Teeple, H. M., "Qumran and the Origin of the Fourth Gospel," *Novum Testamentum* 4 (1960) 6-25

IX. THE QUMRAN CALENDAR AND RELATED PROBLEMS

A. *The Qumran Calendar*

Basic Discussions:

Barthélemy, D., "Notes en marge de publications récentes sur les manuscrits de Qumrân," *RB* 59 (1952) 187-218, esp. pp. 200-2

Jaubert, A., "Le calendrier des Jubilés et de la secte de Qumrân: Ses origines bibliques," *VT* 3 (1955) 250-64

Milik, J. T., "Le travail d'édition des manuscrits du Désert de Juda," *Volume du Congrès, Strasbourg, 1956* (VTSup 4; Leiden: Brill, 1957) 17-26, esp. pp. 24-25

Talmon, S., "The Calendar Reckoning of the Sect from the Judaean Desert," *Aspects of the Dead Sea Scrolls* (Scripta hierosolymitana, 4; Jerusalem: Magnes, 1958) 162-99

Further Discussions:

Baumgarten, J. M., "The Beginning of the Day in the Calendar of Jubilees," *JBL* 77 (1958) 355-60

Baumgarten, J. M., "The Counting of the Sabbath in Ancient Sources," *VT* 16 (1966) 277-86

Beckwith, R. T., "The Modern Attempt to Reconcile the Qumran Calendar with the True Solar Year," *RQ* 7 (1969-71) 379-96

Beckwith, R. T., "The Qumran Calendar and the Sacrifices of the Essenes," *RQ* 7 (1969-71) 587-91

Ettisch, E. E., "Die Gemeinderegel und der Qumrankalender," *RQ* 3 (1961-62) 125-33

Jaubert, A., "Le calendrier des Jubilés et les jours liturgiques de la semaine," *VT* 7 (1957) 35-61

Kimbrough, S. T., "The Concept of Sabbath at Qumran," *RQ* 5 (1964-66) 483-502

Kutsch, E., "Der Kalender des Jubiläenbuches und das Alte und das Neue Testament," *VT* 11 (1961) 39-47

Leach, E. R., "A Possible Method of Intercalation for the Calendar of the Book of Jubilees," *VT* 7 (1957) 392-97

Meysing, J., "L'énigme de la chronologie biblique et qumrânienne dans une nouvelle lumière," *RQ* 6 (1967-69) 229-51

Morgenstern, J., "The Calendar of the Book of Jubilees: Its Origin and Its Character," *VT* 5 (1955) 34-76

Obermann, J., "Calendaric Elements in the Dead Sea Scrolls," *JBL* 75 (1956) 285-97

Strobel, A., "Der 22. Tag des XI. Monats im essenischen Jahr," *RQ* 3 (1961-62) 539-43

Strobel, A., "Zur Funktionsfähigkeit des essenischen Kalenders," *RQ* 3 (1961-62) 395-412

Strobel, A., "Zur kalendarisch-chronologischen Einordnung der Qumran-Essener," *TLZ* 86 (1961) 179-84

Vogt, E., "Antiquum kalendarium sacerdotale," *Bib* 36 (1955) 403-8

Vogt, E., "Kalenderfragmente aus Qumran," *Bib* 39 (1958) 72-77

Wacholder, B. Z., "The Calendar of Sabbatical Cycles during the Second Temple and the Early Rabbinic Period," *HUCA* 44 (1973) 153-96

The Qumran Calendar:

Instead of the luni-solar calendar of 354 days, apparently officially used in the Jerusalem Temple, the Essenes of Qumran employed an older solar calendar of 364 days (see 11QPs^{a} DavComp 27:6, "songs to sing ... for all the days of the year, 364"); cf. *Jubilees* 6:38. For the importance of the calendar, see 1QS 1:14-15; 10:3-8; 1QH 1:15-20; CD 6:18-19; 3:13-15; 16:1-5; 1QpHab 11:4-8 [the latter indicates a difference of calendar being used by the Qumran community and the Wicked Priest of Jerusalem who persecuted them].

Day of the Week	*Months* I, IV, VII, X					II, V, VIII, XI					III, VI, IX, XII				
4 (Wed.)	1	8	15	22	29		6	13	20	27		4	11	18	25
5 (Thur.)	2	9	16	23	30		7	14	21	28		5	12	19	26
6 (Fri.)	3	10	17	24		1	8	15	22	29		6	13	20	27
7 (Sabbath)	4	11	18	25		2	9	16	23	30		7	14	21	28
1 (Sun.)	5	12	19	26		3	10	17	24		1	8	15	22	29
2 (Mon.)	6	13	20	27		4	11	18	25		2	9	16	23	30
3 (Tues.)	7	14	21	28		5	12	19	26		3	10	17	24	31
			(30)					(30)					(31)		

B. *The Qumran Calendar and the Date of Passover in the New Testament*

(1) *The Problem of the Date of the Last Supper*

(a) *Jesus' Death Recorded on the Eve of a Sabbath:*

Mark 15:42 ("when evening had come, since it was the day of Preparation, that is, the day before the Sabbath, Joseph of Arimathea ..."); Matt 27:62 ("Next day, that is, after the day of Preparation"); Luke 23:54 ("It was the day of Preparation, and the Sabbath was beginning" [see 23:56]); John 19:31, 42 ("since it was the day of Preparation, in order to prevent the bodies from remaining on the cross on the Sabbath (for that Sabbath was a high day),...").

Paraskeuē is here understood as the Preparation Day for the Sabbath (= *prosabbaton*).

(b) John 18:28 implies that this *paraskeuē* was the Preparation Day for the Passover -- probably the reason for his parenthetical remark in 19:31, the coincidence of Passover and the beginning of the Sabbath. Hence *paraskeuē* is 14 Nisan (up to sundown [on Friday]). But this would mean that Jesus ate the Last Supper on Thursday, roughly at the beginning of 14 Nisan, a day early. Cf. John 19:14.

(c) Mark 14:12 ("on the first day of Unleavened Bread, when they sacrificed the passover lamb, his disciples said to him, 'Where will you have us go and prepare for you to eat the passover'"); 16 ("they prepared the passover"); cf. Matt 26:17-19; Luke 22:7-13. These passages suggest that Jesus ate the Last Supper as a Passover meal, i.e., prepared on the 14 Nisan, eaten at sundown (roughly), at the beginning of 15 Nisan.

(2) *Solutions of the Problem*

(a) *Theological Solutions:*

The Synoptics place the Last Supper of Jesus with the Twelve at the beginning of 15 Nisan to give it the character of a passover meal (most explicit in Luke 22, but probably also intended in Mark and Matthew as well). John places it on the Preparation Day to depict Jesus slain about the same time as the slaughter of the passover lambs, thus giving his death a special connotation (he dies as the Lamb of God).

(b) *Calendaric Solutions:*

Different calendars were used by the Synoptics and John. Before the discovery of the Qumran calendar, it was often said that the difference was one of Pharisaic and Sadducee calendars, but the evidence for that difference was not really forthcoming. Since the discovery of the Qumran (Essene) calendar, the explanation of two calendars, which were then in use, has been proposed to solve this classic problem of gospel interpretation. It was mainly proposed by A. Jaubert, *La date de la Cène, calendrier biblique et liturgie chrétienne* (Etudes bibliques; Paris; Gabalda, 1957); *The Date of the Last Supper* (Staten Island: Alba House, 1965).

	SOLAR CALENDAR	*LUNI-SOLAR* (official) *CALENDAR*
Tues. --Before Sundown	14 Nisan: Preparation for Passover (Mark 14:12-16)	
About Sundown	15 Nisan: Last Supper (Passover Meal, Mark 14:17-25)	12 Nisan:
Night	Arrest; Interrogation before Annas (Mark 14:53a; John 18:13); Peter's Denial Led to Caiaphas (John 18:24)	
Wed. --Before Sundown	15 Nisan: First Appearance before Sanhedrin (Mark 14:55)	12 Nisan:
At Sundown	16 Nisan:	13 Nisan:
Thurs.--Before Sundown	16 Nisan: Second Appearance before Sanhedrin (Mark 15:1a) Jesus led to Pilate (Mark 15:1b) Jesus sent to Herod (Luke 23:7-11) People stirred up to demand Barabbas' release (Mark 15:11)	13 Nisan:

	At Sundown	17 Nisan:	14 Nisan:
	Night	Dream of Pilate's wife (Matt 27:19)	
Fri.	--Before Sundown	17 Nisan: Jesus led to Pilate again (Luke 23:11) Barabbas released (Mark 15:15 Jesus delivered to be crucified; death (Mark 15:15-37)	14 Nisan: Preparation for Passover (John 18:28)
	At Sundown	18 Nisan: Sabbath Jesus in the tomb (Mark 15:42-46)	15 Nisan: Sabbath and Passover (John 19:31)
Sat.	--Before Sundown	18 Nisan: Sabbath Jesus in the Tomb	15 Nisan: Sabbath

According to this solution, Jesus would have eaten the Last Supper according to the solar calendar (about sundown on 15 Nisan, Tuesday evening) and been crucified according to the luni-solar calendar (on 14 Nisan, the Preparation Day for the passover). Thus the Synoptics dated the Last Supper according to the old solar calendar, and John records his death according to the official calendar.

Initial favorable reactions to the proposed solution came mainly from OT scholars and conservative NT interpreters. Problems with the solution are mainly two: (a) Is there ever an indication elsewhere in the gospel tradition that Jesus followed the solar calendar in opposition to the luni-solar (official) calendar? (b) The harmonization of Synoptic and Johannine material in the proposal rides roughshod over the long-accepted analyses of many of the passages according to form-critical methods and betrays a fundamentalist concern.

Further discussions of the proposal:

Blinzler, J., "Qumran-Kalender und Passionschronologie," *ZNW* 49 (1958) 238-51

Braun, H., *Qumran und das Neue Testament* (see section 10/VIII above), 2. 43-54

Carmignac, J., "Les apparitions de Jésus ressuscité et le calendrier biblico-qumranien," *RQ* 7 (1969-71) 483-504

Carmignac, J., "Comment Jésus et ses contemporains pouvaient-ils célébrer la Pâque à une date non officielle?" *RQ* 5 (1964-66) 59-79

Cortés Quirant, J., "La nueva fecha de la última cena," *Estudios bíblicos* 17 (1958) 47-81

Hoehner, H. W., "Chronological Aspects of the Life of Christ," *Bibliotheca sacra* 131 (1974) 241-64

Jaubert, A., "Le mercredi où Jésus fut livré," *NTS* 14 (1967-68) 145-64

Kuhn, K. G., "Zum essenischen Kalender," *ZNW* 52 (1961) 65-73

Mann, C. S., "The Chronology of the Passion and the Qumran Calendar," *Church Quarterly Review* 160 (1959) 446-56

Ruckstuhl, E., *Chronology of the Last Days of Jesus: A Critical Study* (New York: Desclée, 1965) (a poor translation of *Die Chronologie des letzten Mahles und des Leidens Jesu* (Biblische Beiträge; Einsiedeln: Benziger, 1963)

Skehan, P. W., "The Date of the Last Supper," *CBQ* 20 (1958) 192-99

Strobel, A., "Der Termin des Todes Jesu: Überschau und Lösungsverschlag unter Einschluss des Qumrankalenders," *ZNW* 51 (1960) 69-101

Walker, N., "The Dating of the Last Supper," *JQR* 47 (1957) 293-95

Walther, J. A., "The Chronology of Passion Week," *JBL* 77 (1958) 116-22

X. HISTORY OF THE QUMRAN COMMUNITY

Allegro, J., *The Dead Sea Scrolls: A Reappraisal* (Pelican Books A376; Baltimore: Penguin, 1964) 103-9

Cross, F. M., *ALQ*, 49-160

Denis, A.-M., *Les thèmes de connaissance* (see section 10/V above)

Dupont-Sommer, A., *The Essene Writings from Qumran* (see section 8 above) 339-67

Iwry, S., "Was There a Migration to Damascus? The Problem of *šby yśr'l*," *W. F. Albright Volume* (Eretz Israel, 9; Jerusalem: Israel Exploration Society, 1969) 80-88

Jeremias, G., *Der Lehrer der Gerechtigkeit* (see section 10/V above)

Milik, J. T., *Ten Years* (see section 4 above) 44-97

Murphy-O'Connor, J., "The Essenes and Their History," *RB* 81 (1974) 215-44 (a recent fundamental discussion)

Rabinowitz, I., "Sequence and Dates of the Extra-Biblical Dead Sea Scroll Texts and 'Damascus' Fragments," *VT* 3 (1953) 175-85

Rowley, H. H., "The History of the Qumran Sect," *Bulletin of the John Rylands Library* 49 (1966-67) 203-32

Stegemann, H., *Die Entstehung der Qumrangemeinde* (Dissertation, Bonn, 1965; privately published, 1971) [non vidi]

11

THE COPPER PLAQUE MENTIONING BURIED TREASURE

(3QTreasure, 3Q*15*)

THE COPPER PLAQUE MENTIONING BURIED TREASURE

(3QTreasure, 3Q*15*)

This copper plaque, that is also variously referred to as the "Copper Scroll" or the "Copper Rolls" (because it was found in two parts rolled up to resemble scrolls, but is really not a scroll at all), was found in Qumran Cave 3 in 1952. The archaeological institutions that were involved in the exploration of the cliffs along the northwest shore of the Dead Sea in that year entrusted the publication of it to J. T. Milik. Attempts to open the brittle oxidized copper were unsuccessful; the attempt to restore it to a supple copper form were on the verge of success when it was decided to saw it open in strips at Manchester in England. J. M. Allegro was on the spot at the time and was on the point of publishing the first reading of the text and a translation (see below). Milik's publication of the text in DJD 3 is the official publication of the text and is to be regarded as the *editio princeps*, despite the prior making known of the text to the public by Allegro.

Though it was found in the Qumran Cave 3, it is most likely that it had nothing to do with the Qumran community. It resembles the rest of the Qumran writings neither in palaeography nor in language (being an early form of Mishnaic Hebrew).

3Q Treasure, 3Q*15* Milik, J. T., "Le rouleau de cuivre provenant de la grotte 3 (3Q*15*)," DJD 3. 199-302

See further:

Kuhn, K. G., "Les rouleaux de cuivre de Qumrân," *RB* 61 (1954) 193-205

Kuhn, K. G., "Die Kupferrollen von Qumrân und ihr Inhalt," *TLZ* 79 (1954) 303-4

Milik, J. T., "Le rouleau de cuivre de Qumran (3Q15): Traduction et commentaire topographique," *RB* 66 (1959) 321-57

Milik, J. T., "The Copper Document from Cave III of Qumran: Translation and Commentary," *ADAJ* 4-5 (1960) 137-55

Baker, H. W., "Notes on the Opening of the 'Bronze' Scrolls from Qumran," *Bulletin of the John Rylands Library* 39 (1956) 45-56 (see also DJD 3. 203-10)

Cross, F. M., "Excursus on the Palaeographical Dating of the Copper Document," DJD 3. 217-21

Allegro, J. M., *The Treasure of the Copper Scroll* (Garden City: Doubleday, 1960) (A translation and commentary that are to be used with great caution; see R. de Vaux, *RB* 68 [1961] 146-47; J. A. Fitzmyer, *TS* 22 [1961] 292-96)

Dupont-Somer, A., "Les rouleaux de cuivre trouvés à Qoumrân," *RHR* 151 (1957) 22-35

Jeremias, J., "Remarques sur le rouleau de cuivre de Qumrân," *RB* 67 (1960) 220-22

Jeremias, J., "The Copper Scroll from Qumran," *ExpT* 71 (1959-60) 227-28

Jeremias, J., *The Rediscovery of Bethesda: John 5:2* (NT Archaeology Monograph, 1; Louisville: Southern Baptist Theological Seminary, 1966)

Jeremias, J., *Abba: Studien zur neutestamentlichen Theologie und Zeitgeschichte* (Göttingen: Vandenhoeck & Ruprecht, 1966) 361-64

Kuhn, K. G., "Bericht über neue Qumranfunde und über die Öffnung der Kupferrolle," *TLZ* 81 (1956) 541-46

Lurie, B. Z., *M^egillat han-n^eḥōšet mimmidbar Y^ehûdāh* (Publications of the Israel Bible Research Society, 14; Jerusalem: Kirjath Sepher, 1963)

Milik, J. T., "Notes d'épigraphie et de topographie palestiniennes," *RB* 66 (1959) 550-75, esp. pp. 567-75; 67 (1960) 354-67

Milik, J. T., "Observations," *RB* 67 (1960) 222-23 (on the article of J. Jeremias)

Milik, J. T., "The Copper Document from Cave III, Qumran," *BA* 19 (1956) 532

Mowinckel, S., "The Copper Scroll--An Apocryphon?" *JBL* 76 (1957) 261-65

Silberman, L. H., "A Note on the Copper Scroll," *VT* 10 (1960) 77-79 (see also the postscript by P. Grelot, pp. 37-38)

Dalman, G., "The Search for the Temple Treasure at Jerusalem," *Palestine Exploration Fund Quarterly Statement* 1912-13, pp. 35-39

Addendum

Fr. 6 of 4Q*158* has subsequently been identified by R. Weiss as a Proto-Samaritan form of Ex 20:19ff. See his review in *Kirjath Sepher* 45 (1970) 61.

12

INDEXES

I. INDEX OF MODERN AUTHORS

II. INDEX OF BIBLICAL PASSAGES

The following list not only supplies references to pages in this book (in parentheses on the right) but also gives information as to where one can find the biblical texts that are quoted in the Dead Sea Scrolls. Included are not only such texts as 1QIsa[a], 1QIsa[b], 11QPs[a], (with their detailed listings), but also the isolated quotations of the OT in various scrolls. For the psalter in Qumran writings, one should consult J. A. Sanders, *DSPS*, 146-49; his list is fuller than that given below for the Psalms, because he also lists the Psalms that are known to exist but that have not yet been published. The list of psalm-passages given below is limited to those that have been published. In the following list, col. 1 gives the passages of biblical books, col. 2 the commonly used Qumran (Murabbaʿat, etc.) siglum, col. 3 the numbered siglum in the DJD series, and col. 4 the page(s) of this book on which the full information is given where the Qumran (or Murabbaʿat, etc.) text in question can be found.

Genesis

1:18-21	1QGen	1Q*1*	(15)
1:27	CD 4:19-5:2		(53)
3:11-14	1QGen	1Q*1*	(15)
6:8-9	1QapGen		(14)
6:13-21	6QpaleoGen	6Q*1*	(20)
7:9	CD 4:19-5:2		(53)
9:2-3, 4, 20	1QapGen		(14)
10:6, 20	6QGen(?) ar	6Q*19*	(21)
12:8-15:4	1QapGen		(14)
17:12-19	8QGen	8Q*1*	(22)
19:27-28	2QGen	2Q*1*	(18)
22:13-15	1QGen	1Q*1*	(15)
23:17-19	1QGen	1Q*1*	(15)
24:22-24	1QGen	1Q*1*	(15)
25:9, 7-8	2QJub[a]	2Q*19*	(19)
28:10, 11	1QJub[a]	1Q*17*	(16)
32:4-5, 30	MurGen	Mur 1	(41)
32:25-32, 31(?)	4QBibParaph	4Q*158*	(33)
32:33-33:1	MurGen	Mur 1	(41)

34:5-7	MurGen	Mur 1	(41)
34:30-35:1, 4-7	MurGen	Mur 1	(41)
35:6-10	?ḤevGen		(46)
36:5-12	?ḤevGen		(46)
36:6, 35-37	2QGen	2Q*1*	(18)
46:7-11	MasGen		(40)
50:26, 22	2QJub[b]	2Q*20*	(19)

Exodus

1:1-5	4QExod[a]		(23)
1:7	2QJub[b]	2Q*20*	(19)
1:11-14	2QExod[a]	2Q*2*	(18)
3:12	4QBibParaph	4Q*158*	(33)
4:27-28	4QBibParaph	4Q*158*	(33)
4:28-31	MurExod	Mur 1	(41)
4:31	2QExod[b]	2Q*3*	(18)
5:3	MurExod	Mur 1	(41)
5:3-5	2QExod[c]	2Q*4*	(18)
6:5-11	MurExod	Mur 1	(41)
6:25-7:19	4QpaleoExod[m]		(23)
7:1-4	2QExod[a]	2Q*2*	(18)
9:27-29	2QExod[a]	2Q*2*	(18)
11:3-7	2QExod[a]	2Q*2*	(18)
12:26-27(?)	2QExod[b]	2Q*3*	(18)
12:32-41	2QExod[a]	2Q*2*	(18)
13:1-10, 11-16	MurPhyl	Mur 4	(41)
13:2-3, 7-9	1QPhyl	1Q*13*	(15)
15:1b-18	4QExod[c]		(23)
15:17-18	4QFlor	4Q*174*	(28, 33)
16:12-16	1QExod	1Q*2*	(15)
18:21-22	2QExod[b]	2Q*3*	(18)
19:9	2QExod[b]	2Q*3*	(18)
19:17-23	4QBibParaph	4Q*158*	(33)
19:24-20:1	1QExod	1Q*2*	(15)
20:5-6	1QExod	1Q*2*	(15)
20:12, 16, 17	4QBibParaph	4Q*158*	(33)
20:19-22 (Sam.)	4QBibParaph	4Q*158* fr. 6	(33, 143)

20:2-3	11QpaleoLev		(35)
20:20-24	1QLev	1Q*3*	(15)
21:6-9	11QpaleoLev		(35)
21:24-22:6	1QLev	1Q*3*	(15)
22:22-25	11QpaleoLev		(35)
23:1-3	2QNum[d(?)]	2Q*9*	(18)
23:4-8	1QLev	1Q*3*	(15)
23:38	CD 11:17-18		(53)
24:9-10	11QpaleoLev		(35)
25:9	11QMelch 26		(36)
25:10	11QMelch 6		(36)
25:13	11QMelch 2		(36)
25:29-35	11QpaleoLev		(35)
26:2-16	4QLXX Lev[a]		(25)
26:20-24	11QpaleoLev		(35)
27:13-17	11QpaleoLev		(35)
27:30-31(?)	1QLev	1Q*3*	(15)

Numbers

1:48-50	1QLev	1Q*3*	(15)
3:38-41	2QNum[a]	2Q*6*	(18)
3:40-42	4QLXX Num		(25)
3:51-4:3	2QNum[a]	2Q*6*	(18)
4:6-9	4QLXX Num		(25)
7:88	2QNum[c]	2Q*8*	(18)
10:9	1QM 10:6-8		(14)
18:8-9	2QNum[d(?)]	2Q*9*	(18)
20:7-8	5/6ḤevNum		(46)
21:18	CD 6:3-11		(53)
24:15-17	4QTestim	4Q*175*	(28, 33)
24:17	CD 7:18-21		(53)
24:17-19	1QM 11:5-7		(14)
30:17	CD 7:8-9		(53)
33:47-53	2QNum[b]	2Q*7*	(18)
34:10	MurNum	Mur 1	(41)
36:7-8	1QLev	1Q*3*	(15)
36:7-11	MurNum	Mur 1	(41)

Deuteronomy

15:2	11QMelch 3		(36)
15:14-15	1QDeut[b]	*1Q5*	(15)
16:4, 6-7	1QDeut[a]	*1Q4*	(15)
17:12-15	2QDeut[b]	*2Q11*	(18)
17:16	1QDeut[b]	*1Q5*	(15)
17:17	CD 4:19-5:2		(53)
18:18-19	4QTestim	*4Q175*	(28, 33)
18:18-20, 22	4QBibParaph	*4Q158*	(33)
20:2-5	1QM 10:2-5		(14)
21:8-9	1QDeut[b]	*1Q5*	(15)
23:24	CD 16:6-7		(53)
24:10-16	1QDeut[b]	*1Q5*	(15)
25:13-18	1QDeut[b]	*1Q5*	(15)
26:19(?)	6QDeut	*6Q3*	(21)
28:44-48	1QDeut[b]	*1Q5*	(15)
29:9-11, 12-20	1QDeut[b]	*1Q5*	(15)
30:19-31:6, 7-10, 12-13	1QDeut[b]	*1Q5*	(15)
32:17-21, 21-22, 22-29, 24-25	1QDeut[b]	*1Q5*	(15)
32:33	CD 8:9-12		(53)
32:37-43	4QDeut[q]		(23)
33:8-11	4QTestim	*4Q175*	(28, 33)
33:8-11, 12(?), 19-21	4QFlor	*4Q174*	(33)
33:12-17, 18-19, 21-23, 24	1QDeut[b]	*1Q5*	(15)

Joshua

6:26	4QTestim	*4Q175*	(28, 33)

Judges

6:20-22	1QJudg	*1Q6*	(15)
8:1	1QJudg	*1Q6*	(15)
9:1-4, 4-6, 28-31, 40-42, 40-43, 48-49	1QJudg	*1Q6*	(15)

1 Chronicles

17:9-13	4QFlor	*4Q174*	(33)

Job

33:28-30	2QJob	*2Q15*	(19)

Psalms

	4QPs^{a-q}		(25)
1:1	4QFlor	*4Q174*	(33)
2:1	4QFlor	*4Q174*	(33)
2:6-7	3QPs	*3Q2*	(19)
7:8-9	11QMelch 10		(36)
7:14-31:22	5/6ḤevPs		(46)
15:1-5	5/6ḤevPs		(46)
16:1	5/6ḤevPs		(46)
17:5-9, 14	8QPs	*8Q2*	(22)
18:6-9, 10-13	8QPs	*8Q2*	(22)
31:24-25	4QPs^{q}		(24)
33:1-18	4QPs^{q}		(24)
35:4-20	4QPs^{q}		(24)
37:7, 8-19a, 19b-26, 28c-40	4QPs^{a}	*4Q171*	(33)
44:3-5, 4, 7, 9, 23-24, 25	1QPs^{c}	*1Q12*	(15)
45:1-2	4QpPs^{a}	*4Q171*	(33)
57:1, 4	1QpPs	*1Q16*	(16)
60:8-9	4QpPs^{a}	*4Q171*	(33)
68:12-13, 26-27, 30-31	1QpPs	*1Q16*	(16)
78:36-37(?)	6QPs	*6Q5*	(21)
79:2-3	4QTanḥumim	*4Q176*	(28, 34)
81:3-85:10	MasPs		(40)
82:1	11QMelch 10		(36)
82:2	11QMelch 11		(36)
86:5-8	1QPs^{a}	*1Q10*	(15)
89:20-31	4QPs89	*4Q236*	(25)
91:1-16	11QPsAp^{a}		(35)

119:1-6	11QPs^{a} col. vi		(38)
119:15-28	11QPs^{a} col. vii		(38)
119:31-34, 43-48, 77-79	1QPs^{a}	1Q*10*	(15)
119:37-49	11QPs^{a} col. viii		(38)
119:59-73	11QPs^{a} col. ix		(38)
119:82-96	11QPs^{a} col. x		(38)
119:99-101, 104, 113-20, 138-42	5QPs	5Q*5*	(20)
119:105-20	11QPs^{a} col. xi		(38)
119:128-42	11QPs^{a} col. xii		(38)
119:150-64	11QPs^{a} col. xiii		(38)
119:171-76	11QPs^{a} col. xiv		(38)
121:1-8	11QPs^{a} col. iii		(38)
122:1-9	11QPs^{a} col. iii		(38)
123:1-2	11QPs^{a} col. iii		(38)
124:7-8	11QPs^{a} col. iv		(38)
125:1-5	11QPs^{a} col. iv		(38)
126:1-6	11QPs^{a} col. iv		(38)
126:6	1QPs^{b}	1Q*11*	(15)
127:1	11QPs^{a} col. iv		(38)
127:1-5	1QPs^{b}	1Q*11*	(15)
127:2-3, 5	4QpPs^{b}	4Q*173*	(33)
128:4-6	11QPs^{a} col. v		(38)
129:1-8	11QPs^{a} col. v		(38)
129:7-8	4QpPs^{b}	4Q*173*	(33)
130:1-8	11QPs^{a} col. v		(38)
131:1	11QPs^{a} col. v		(38)
132:8-18	11QPs^{a} col. vi		(38)
133:1-3	11QPs^{a} col. xxiii		(38)
133:1-3	11QPs^{b}		(35)
134:1-3	11QPs^{a} col. xxviii		(38)
135:1-9	11QPs^{a} col. xiv		(38)
135:17-21	11QPs^{a} col. xv		(38)
136:1-16	11QPs^{a} col. xv		(38)
136:26b(?)	11QPs^{a} col. xvi		(38)
137:1	11QPs^{a} col. xx		(38)

Isaiah

1-66	1QIsa[a]		(11)
?	1QIsa[b]	1Q*8* fr. 7	(13)
1:1	3QpIsa	3Q*4*	(19)
1:1(?)	4QpIsa[e]	4Q*165*	(33)
1:4-14	MurIsa	Mur 3	(41)
2:22	1QS 5:17-18		(14)
5:5-6, 11-14, 24-25, 29-30	4QpIsa[b]	4Q*162*	(33)
6:9(?)	4QpIsa[b]	4Q*162*	(33)
7:17	CD 7:10-12		(53)
7:22-8:1	1QIsa[b]	1Q*8* 1:1-8	(12, 15)
8:7, 8, 9(?)	4QpIsa[c]	4Q*163*	(33)
8:11	4QFlor 1:14-16		(28, 33)
8:11	4QFlor	4Q*174*	(33)
9:11(?), 14-20	4QpIsa[c]	4Q*163*	(33)
10:12, 13, 19(?), 20-24	4QpIsa[c]	4Q*163*	(33)
10:17-19	1QIsa[b]	*DSSHU* fr. 1	(12)
10:20-21, 22, 24-27, 28-32, 33-34	4QpIsa[a]	4Q*161*	(33)
11:1-5	4QpIsa[a]	4Q*161*	(33)
12:3-13:8	1QIsa[b]	1Q*8* 2:1-9	(12, 15)
12:5-13:6	4QIsa[a]		(24)
13:16-19	1QIsa[b]	*DSSHU* fr. 2	(12)
14:8, 26-30	4QpIsa[c]	4Q*163*	(33)
14:19	4QpIsa[e]	4Q*165*	(33)
15:3-16:2	1QIsa[b]	1Q*8* 3:1-10	(12, 15)
15:4-6	4QpIsa[e]	4Q*165*	(33)
16:7-11	1QIsa[b]	*DSSHU* fr. 3	(12)
19:7-17	1QIsa[b]	1Q*8* 4:1-10	(12, 15)
19:9-12	4QpIsa[c]	4Q*163*	(33)
19:20-20:1	1QIsa[b]	*DSSHU* fr. 4	(12)
21:2(?), 11-15	4QpIsa[e]	4Q*165*	(33)
22:11-18	1QIsa[b]	1Q*8* 5:1-10	(12, 15)
22:13d-23:6a	4QIsa[a]		(24)
22:24-23:4	1QIsa[b]	*DSSHU* fr. 5	(12)

49:7, 13-17	4QTanḥumim	4Q*176*	(28, 34)
50:7-11	1QIsa^{b}	*DSSHU* col. 7	(13)
51:1-10	1QIsa^{b}	*DSSHU* col. 7	(13)
51:22-23, 23c-e	4QTanḥumim	4Q*176*	(28, 34)
52:1-2	4QTanḥumim	4Q*176*	(28, 34)
52:1-3	4QTanḥumim	4Q*176*	(28, 34)
52:7	11QMelch 15		(36)
52:7-15	1QIsa^{b}	*DSSHU* col. 8	(13)
53:1-12	1QIsa^{b}	*DSSHU* col. 8	(13)
54:1-6	1QIsa^{b}	*DSSHU* col. 8	(13)
54:4-10	4QTanḥumim	4Q*176*	(28, 34)
54:11, 12	4QpIsa^{d}	4Q*164*	(33)
54:16	CD 6:3-11		(53)
55:2-13	1QIsa^{b}	*DSSHU* col. 9	(13)
56:1-12	1QIsa^{b}	*DSSHU* col. 9	(13)
57:1-4	1QIsa^{b}	*DSSHU* col. 9	(13)
57:17-21	1QIsa^{b}	*DSSHU* col. 10	(13)
58:1-14	1QIsa^{b}	*DSSHU* col. 10	(13)
59:1-8	1QIsa^{b}	*DSSHU* col. 10	(13)
59:20-21	1QIsa^{b}	*DSSHU* col. 11	(13)
60:1-22	1QIsa^{b}	*DSSHU* col. 11	(13)
61:1	11QMelch 4		(36)
61:1-2	1QIsa^{b}	*DSSHU* col. 11	(13)
62:2-12	1QIsa^{b}	*DSSHU* col. 12	(13)
63:1-19	1QIsa^{b}	*DSSHU* col. 12	(13)
64:1, 6-8	1QIsa^{b}	*DSSHU* col. 12	(13)
65:17-25	1QIsa^{b}	*DSSHU* col. 13	(13)
66:1-24	1QIsa^{b}	*DSSHU* col. 13	(13)

Jeremiah

7:29-9:2	4QJer^{a}		(24)
9:7-14	4QJer^{a}		(24)
9:22-10:18	4QJer^{b}		(24)
10:4, 9, 11	4QJer^{b}		(24)
10:9-14	4QJer^{a}		(24)
11:3-6	4QJer^{a}		(24)
12:3-6	4QJer^{a}		(24)

Daniel

1:10-17	1QDan[a]	1Q*71*	(13, 15)
2:2-6	1QDan[a]	1Q*71*	(13, 15)
3:22-28, 27-30	1QDan[b]	1Q*72*	(13, 15)
8:16-17(?)	6QDan	6Q*7*	(21)
8:20-21(?)	6QDan	6Q*7*	(21)
10:8-16	6QDan	6Q*7*	(21)
11:32	4QFlor	4Q*174*	(33)
11:33-36, 38	6QDan	6Q*7*	(21)
12:10	4QFlor	4Q*174*	(33)

Hosea

1:7-2:5	4QXII[d]		(25)
2:8-9, 10-14	4QpHos[a]	4Q*166*	(33)
3:4	CD 20:15-17		(53)
4:16	CD 1:13-14		(53)
5:10	CD 19:15-16		(53)
5:13-15	4QpHos[b]	4Q*167*	(33)
6:4, 7, 9-10	4QpHos[b]	4Q*167*	(33)
6:9	4QpIsa[c]	4Q*163*	(33)
8:13-14	4QpHos[b]	4Q*167*	(33)
13:15b-14a, 3-6	4QXII(?)		(24)

Joel

2:20	MurXII	Mur 88 i	(41)
2:26-4:16	MurXII	Mur 88 ii	(41)

Amos

1:3-5	5QAmos	5Q*4*	(20)
1:5(?)	8ḤevXII gr fr. 2		(47)
1:5-2:1	MurXII	Mur 88 iii	(41)
5:26-27	CD 7:14-15		(53)
6	MurXII	Mur 88 vi	(42)
7:3-8:7	MurXII	Mur 88 vii	(42)
8:11-9:15	MurXII	Mur 88 viii	(42)
9:11	4QFlor	4Q*174*	(33)
9:11	CD 7:15-16		(53)
9:11	4QFlor 1-3 ii 11-13		(28, 33)

1:13-14	8ḤevXII gr fr. 5		(47)
1:14	8ḤevXII gr fr. 3		(47)
2:5-14	8ḤevXII gr col. ix		(46)
2:12	MurXII	Mur 88 xvi	(42)
2:12-14	4QpNah	4Q*169*	(33)
2:13-3:19	MurXII	Mur 88 xvii	(42)
3:1-5, 6-9, 10-12, 14	4QpNah	4Q*169*	(33)
3:3	8ḤevXII gr fr. 8		(47)
3:16-17	8ḤevXII gr col. x		(46)
3:13	8ḤevXII gr fr. 1		(47)

Habakkuk

1:2-17	1QpHab		(14)
1:3-2:11	MurXII	Mur 88 xviii	(42)
1:5-11	8ḤevXII gr col. xi		(46)
1:14-17	8ḤevXII gr col. xii		(46)
2:1-8	8ḤevXII gr col. xii		(46)
2:1-20	1QpHab		(14)
2:13-20	8ḤevXII gr col. xiii		(46)
2:18	MurXII	Mur 88 xix	(42)
3:9-15	8ḤevXII gr col. xiv		(47)

Zephaniah

1:1	MurXII	Mur 88 xix	(42)
1:1-5	8ḤevXII gr col. xv		(47)
1:11-3:6	MurXII	Mur 88 xx	(42)
1:12-13	4QpZeph	4Q*170*	(33)
1:13-17	8ḤevXII gr col. xvi		(47)
1:18-2:2	1QpZeph	1Q*15*	(16)
2:9-10	8ḤevXII gr col. xvii		(47)
3:6-7	8ḤevXII gr col. xviii		(47)
3:8	MurXII	Mur 88 xxi	(42)

Haggai

1:11	MurXII	Mur 88 xxi	(42)
1:12-2:10	MurXII	Mur 88 xxii	(42)
2:12	MurXII	Mur 88 xxiii	(42)

Zechariah

1:1, 3-4	8ḤevXII gr col. xix		(47)
1:4	MurXII	Mur 88 xxiii	(42)
1:13-14	8ḤevXII gr col. xx		(47)
2:2, 7	8ḤevXII gr col. xxi		(47)
2:11-12	8ḤevXII gr fr. 9		(47)
2:16-17	8ḤevXII gr col. xxii		(47)
3:1, 4-7	8ḤevXII gr col. xxii		(47)
3:1-2	8ḤevXII gr fr. 7		(47)
8:19-23	8ḤevXII gr col. xxiii		(47)
8:24-9:4	8ḤevXII gr col. xxiv		(47)
11:11	4QpIsa[c]	4Q*163*	(33)
13:7	CD 19:7-9		(53)
13:9	4QTanḥumim	4Q*176*	(28, 34)

Malachi

1:10	CD 6:11-14		(53)
1:13-14	5QapMal	5Q*10*	(20)

Sirach

1:19-20(?)	2QSir	2Q*18*	(19)
6:14-15(?)	2QSir	2Q*18*	(19)
6:20-31	2QSir	2Q*18*	(19)
39:27-44:17c	MasSir		(40)
51:13-20b	11QPs[a]	col. xxi	(38)
51:30	11QPs[a]	col. xxii	(38)

Epistle of Jeremiah

43-44	7QEpJer gr	7Q*2*	(21)

Acts

10:28-29, 32-41	Mird Acts cpa		(52)

NEW TESTAMENT PASSAGES REFERRED TO